Start Your Own Screen Printing Business

Start Your Own Screen Printing Business

A Users Guide to Printing and Selling T-shirts

by

Anthony Mongiello and Charese Mongiello

iUniverse, Inc.
New York   Bloomington

Start Your Own Screen-Printing Business
A User's Guide to Printing and Selling T-shirts

Editor: Henry Trombley
Layout and Artwork: Drew McCartney

iUniverse books may be ordered through booksellers or by contacting:

iUniverse
1663 Liberty Drive
Bloomington, IN 47403
www.iuniverse.com
1-800-Authors (1-800-288-4677)

ISBN: 978-0-595-47864-4 (pbk)
ISBN: 978-0-595-71572-5 (cloth)

Printed in the United States of America

To our loving mother,
Joan Mongiello

Contents

Preface

After 2 years of successfully printing and selling shirts, our parents moved to California. Instead of taking their equipment with them, they decided to sell it and buy new equipment in California. The equipment sold immediately. Many past customers were disappointed they did not hear the equipment was for sale until it was already gone. Our father and mother saw the need for silkscreen equipment and because of their extensive knowledge in running a business they immediately thought about helping new people, learn how easy it was to make money in the screen printing business. The biggest block was they did not know how to silk screen. They quickly found the simplest way to show them how easy it is. With the family business we have taught over 6000 people how to silk screen. After over 20 years in the business of helping people beginners, novice, and advanced, start and run their own screen printing business. We saw a clear need for this information on how to silkscreen to be published in a simple comprehensive text. This text was developed from this knowledge and understanding of teaching people to silk screen. We understand it is one thing to teach people and another to do. This text will give you the knowledge and the practical application to silk screen.

Introduction

Dear Reader,

This book was written to help all silk screeners we met over the years get a solid foundation of how to silk screen, sell their products, and get the resources necessary. To help beginners understand the process of silk screening as well as successfully make money doing it. The tips included are optional, but we feel throughout the years that just reading something and not having practical actions to take is not enough. The best knowledge is gained by doing. These exercises are here to give you a way to practice this process. So Welcome to the exciting world of screen-printing. It is one of the last home-based businesses that can be started with little initial investment and very little training. This book is designed to show you how much fun and easy it is to print t-shirts and make money doing it. Remember you do not have to be an artist or have a business mindset to be successful at running a silk-screening business. "Start Your Own Screen Printing Business" can show you how to do these things the simple way. And we have watched thousands of people become successful entrepreneurs with silk-screening who have never printed a t-shirt before in their life. Having the knowledge to have your own successful home based business is just a few pages away. Our hope is that from reading this book you too, will have all the knowledge necessary to be successful at this endeavor.

Chapter 1

—

Is There a Market and How Much Can Be Made With T-shirts?

Everywhere you look there are printed t-shirts, creative prints or simply a printed logo to designate a business. Any way you look at it, it means there is money to make advertising someone's business or latest fad. Advertising with t-shirts works! It has proven to be one of the most effective ways to get a message out, with hundreds or even thousands of walking billboards that your advertisers pay you for! It does not get better than that.

For the last 25 years we watched the industry grow each year with the demand for printed t-shirts increasing to all time highs according to industry statistics. All you really need to ask is how many t-shirts do I have and who wears t-shirts? Do not limit yourself to t-shirts; there are sweatshirts, jackets, and polo's. With the increasing market, as you become more advanced you can get into stickers, signs, pillow cases, curtains, jeans, and much more.

Let us take a look at the money to be made, the profits from silk-screening. Initial set up takes one hour total and twenty five dollars for each color (you must charge a set up fee for every order you take). Most of this $25.00 is reclaimable for use in another print. After this, it takes about one minute to print a shirt and five cents for the ink. Shirts cost anywhere from sixty cents to $2.00 and up depending on where you go and what kind of shirts you want; more on this later. For our purposes it is best to stay with the regular high quality t-shirt at $2.00, the highest price for a white shirt. You sell the shirt for $8.00 each shirt with a minimum two dozen. That's a $5.95 profit from each shirt. For every additional color you print you will charge 50 cents to $1.00 more. You will also charge extra for colored shirts. And remember to charge for the set up fee of $25.00 for each color. With a small minimum order of twenty-four t-shirts you have worked about an hour for set up and a half-hour to print the shirts and you made a minimum of $140.00 profit after all the expenses. The profits are all up from there because you have reorders and people telling their friends. Also I would like to say that I have never had anyone only order 24 shirts it is more like 100 or 200 shirts.

We will go into more detail on how to find customers in the later chapters I just wanted to get you started knowing that there are profits right from the beginning and the profits can become pretty high with thousands of shirts being ordered a week. Most silk screeners who have been doing this for a couple of years cannot print fast enough.

Exercise

Go to a copy place and print out a thousand business cards for $10.00 that say you print t-shirts with your name and number on it. When you go to the store or bank and see people you know say "hey I am learning how to print t-shirts if you ever need anything keep me in mind" hand them a card and you will get calls.

If this step is too much for you then just mention that you are learning to print t-shirts to a couple of your close friends who have your number. Tell them you are reading a book on it. I guarantee if you tell at least twenty people you will get someone saying they know someone or they themselves need t-shirt or at least have a good conversation about it.

Chapter 2

–

Terms and Understanding the Printing Process

In this chapter we will go over the basic terms and materials you will need to print t-shirts.

Artwork is the starting point of screen-printing. The first step to a final printed t-shirt is obtaining or making the artwork of the desired print. We will show you later how to obtain the right artwork for printing t-shirts. It is important that you know now that you do not need to be an artist to print t-shirts.

Silkscreen is a square metal or wooden frame with a screen like mesh.

Mesh is the screen like material that goes on the screen. It has a certain amount of holes in it per square inch from 60 to 320. These holes allow ink to go through the screen onto the t-shirt in varying quantity and detail.

Emulsion is like a glue that when put on the screen and dried in a dark room (this is very important) it blocks the holes and prevents the ink from getting through to the t-shirt.

Halogen Light is used to permanently dry the emulsion on the screen so no ink can go through the screen. It is what is used to burn the screen or put the artwork on the screen so that only the holes where the art work will let the ink go through the screen.

Burning a Screen is the process of using the halogen light to put the artwork in the screen so that there is a stencil of the artwork in the screen.

Screen Block is used after you burn the screen to plug up remaining small holes you do not want ink to get through in your screen.

Squeegee is a twelve to sixteen inch handle with a special kind of rubber on it that is used to pull the ink evenly across the screen and push it through the holes onto the shirt.

Coating the Screen is putting the emulsion on the screen prior to burning the artwork in the screen.

Screen Coater is an L shaped instrument used to put the emulsion evenly on the screen to coat the screen with emulsion.

Register the screen(s) is to line the artwork in the screen up with the t-shirts so that you can print in the middle or the same place on each shirt every time. This term also refers to more than one color printing where you line each screen (also known as color) up with each other so that they do not over lap. They fit just right just like when you see the artwork on paper. This process is only done with silkscreen machines and this is why people buy them.

All of these terms and there uses and processes will be explained in further detail in the following chapters please refer back to this if needed.

Exercise

In the back of the book there is a list of suppliers purchase one of each supply mentioned, so you know what they look like or go to our website and purchase a basic supply kit it has one of each item in it, or go online and find pictures of the supplies. You will need this for the next chapter. If this is too much for you, go online to our website www.homecashbusiness.com and check-out these things and get familiar with them.

Chapter 3

—

Silk-screens

This chapter on silk-screens goes into detail about what a silk-screen is and the process of burning a screen.

Mesh Count

When you buy a screen from a screen-printing supply store you simply get a polyester mesh of various degrees of fineness glued to a wooden or aluminum frame. The amount of holes per inch or the mesh (the fineness) is called the mesh count. The higher the mesh count, the more holes per square inch are in the mesh, and the less ink will pass through the screen. Higher mesh counts are used for more detailed prints with finer lines or smaller dots (such as with 4-color processed color prints).

Some examples of what mesh counts are good for what types of prints are given here:

Thick coverage on a dark t-shirt	60
Underbase for a dark T-shirt	86-125
More detailed underbase for a dark T-shirt	160-220
Regular printing on a light T-shirt	110-140
Multicolor printing on a light T-shirt	140-200
Extra detailed printing for a light T-shirt	210-260
Four-Color Process	280-310
Printing on an underbase	280-310
Puff Ink	60-86
Metallic Ink	60-86

Probably the most common error for beginning printers is using the wrong mesh count for the job. Using the wrong mesh count can make burning the image on the screen impossible (too low of a mesh count), or make it impossible to get enough ink onto the t-shirt (too high of a mesh count).

Wooden Frames vs. Retensionable Aluminum

Wooden silkscreen frames are ideal for simpler prints because of their inexpensive price. You can get wooden silk screens for around $15 - $20, and for the average print it will be more than adequate for getting the job done. As the job gets harder, more detailed aluminum screens become the only way to ensure a high quality print. Aluminum retensionable frames are good because as the screen fabric becomes worn down from use it becomes loose(on wooden screens), which causes the screen to not register as well as it used to. When this happens with a wooden screen they are no longer good for multicolored prints, but with a aluminum retensionable screen your retention in the screen sometimes becomes even tighter than when it was new making it literally better than new. The tighter the screen fabric is stretched the better the screen will register.

Degreasing the Screen

Before you can coat a screen you must first degrease it. This will insure proper burning and wash out. To degrease a screen you simply apply degreaser to the fabric of the screen, scrub with a rag or sponge, and rinse thoroughly. You can apply the degreaser with a spray bottle or pour it on directly, or apply it to your rag or sponge. Degreaser can be obtained at your local screen-printing supply store. You may however prefer to buy degreaser from your local hardware store, and industrial degreaser will work fine. Avoid the use of dishwashing soap and scouring powders as they have substances that could imbed in the fabric of your screen. Please note that you should degrease your screen before every coating.

Coating the Screen

Coating a screen simply means to apply emulsion over the center portion of the fabric of the screen. To do this you use a scoop coater. A scoop coater is an "L" shaped aluminum tool that is slightly shorter than the inside of the frame of your screen. Before opening your emulsion you need to be in a room that is free from ultraviolet light, that is, sunlight, florescent lights of any kind, halogen lights, and mercury vapor lights. To light your room you may use a common household light bulb(60, 75, 100watt). A good test to see if you have too much UV (Ultra Violet) light coming in is to shut off all lights and check if you can still see things clearly with any light coming in through window shades or from the bottom of the door. If you're having trouble sealing off an area from sunlight it may be good to wait for dark and then coat and burn your screens. Once you have your area free from UV light you can begin to coat your screen. First fill the reservoir of the scoop coater with emulsion about half way. Then take the screen and hold it slightly tilted and press the smooth edge of the scoop coater up against the bottom fabric of the screen (about 2 inches from the bottom of the frame). Now tilt the scoop coater so that the emulsion comes into contact with the fabric along the entire length of the scoop coater. Slowly pull the scoop coater up to the top of the screen holding it against the fabric all the way up to about 2 inches from the top of the frame. This should leave a nice even coat. If not, do this again until you have the emulsion evenly distributed on the screen. Now flip the screen over and coat the other side. You can get a thicker coat by redoing the front side (the side that touches the t-shirt or that is flat not indented) once more. For most print jobs coating the front, the back and, the front once more to get a nice thick and even coat over the screen will produce excellent image quality and a great professional looking print. It is not necessary to coat all the fabric on the screen. You can leave about 1- 4 inches of fabric uncoated next to the frame of the screen. It is only really necessary to coat a portion large enough to fit your image on. The rest of the screen can be blocked off with screen block, or for jobs of about four hundred shirts or less, with tape. After the screen is coated it must be stored in a dark place to dry. Store them flat and print side down (squeegee side up). Doing this will increase print quality because the emulsion will dry out in front of polyester filament and produce sharper edges and better line detail. A closet, or a large closed cardboard box or a cabinet do nicely for storing coated screens.

Burning Screens

Burning screens means to put an image (the artwork) onto a screen by placing it under a UV light source. To burn an image using a light source from above, place a coated screen (you still have to be in an area free from UV light) on a table covered with black cloth or cardboard. This will minimize light reflection from your UV light source. Place your image(or artwork) backwards (If you have words make sure you have the artwork is laying on the screen so that the words are unreadable as it will print opposite). (We will go more in detail about what kind of paper the artwork is on and how to get it but for now you will have your artwork on a vellum or clear positive paper) Place a thick piece of glass over the clear positive or vellum piece to keep it pressed tightly to the fabric. It is a good idea to get a piece of glass that is smaller than the inside of the frame of your screens so that it will be able to keep the artwork flatter against the fabric and ensure a crisper image is burned. Also be sure not to have the edge of the glass covering any part of the image as it usually blocks the light and makes lines in the emulsion. By now you will have figured out that the emulsion on the screen gets cured or hardened when under the light and where the artwork blocks the light, the emulsion underneath will wash out. The holes in the screen left open will let the ink go through the screen onto the shirt. The next step is to turn on the light source and burn the screen.

The amount of time will vary with the kind of emulsion you get and the particular light source you have. It is good to keep your light source about 20 inches away from the screen to make sure it gets burned evenly.

Here are some examples of time needed to burn with various light sources:

Light Source	Mesh Counts			
	30-100	120-200	200-300	300-350
500 Watts	4-6 min.	3.5-5min.	3-4 min.	3 min.
1000 Watts	2-3 min.	2-3 min.	1.5-2 min.	1-2 min.
5000 Watts	60-75 sec.	45 sec.	40 sec.	35 sec.
Sunlight	45-60 sec.	30 sec.	25 sec.	20 sec.

Please note that dyed mesh (such as yellow or orange) will take about 25% more time to burn than just plain white mesh. These times are not set in stone your particular light and emulsion may vary considerable from these printed times. Use these as a guideline and go up and down according to how much of your image did or did not wash out.

A good tool to help you find the right amount of exposure time is an exposure calculator. This is a clear plastic sheet with various half tones shades and line thickness printed on it. You burn a screen using the exposure calculator and wash it out to see what washes out. The calculator will give you an idea of what exposure time is just right for your particular screens and light source.

Washing Out

Washing out a screen means to run water over a burned screen and allow the image to come through. When you burn a screen you are making the light sensitive emulsion become hard everywhere but where your image is (the image on the velum or clear positive does not let the light hit the emulsion underneath it). When you run water over it, the emulsion where the image blocked the light will wash away.

A good method for washing out a screen is to spray the screen with water with a light mist all over, front and back, as soon as its done burning. Then take it to your wash out station (for beginners this is the back yard with a hose or their bathtub) and proceed to run water over the screen until the image washes out. Make sure to rinse both sides of the screen with water thoroughly. Failing to do this might cause residue from one side to drip down and clog the fabric where the image is washed out. Be sure not to try and wash a screen out in sunlight, as it will just burn the entire screen before you can wash the image out. If some areas of the screen are not washing out easily you can try increasing the water pressure, but be careful as too much water pressure will blow out even the burned emulsion. If the image does not wash out at all this usually means that you over exposed the screen or that the print on your clear positive or velum is too thin (not dark enough). If all the emulsion comes off this means that you have under exposed the screen. Adjust your burn time until you get a nice crisp image burned in your screen. Make sure to write down the time so that you will remember it for the rest of the screens you burn.

Once the screen is washed out you will want to post expose it if you are doing a lot of shirts. This will harden the emulsion onto the screen really well and make sure that the emulsion does not flake off while you are cleaning it. To post expose just put the screen back under your light source and leave it on for ten minutes. Another way to post expose is to leave the screen out in the sunlight for about 15 minutes because this will dry the screen and post expose it at the same time.

Screen Blocking

Once your screen is dry you will want to screen block it. Screen block is just a thick glue like substance that washes away with water. It is used to block any little pinholes that are in the emulsion where they should not be. To apply screen block, just use a small paintbrush or thin piece of cardboard. Screen block takes about 20 minutes to dry.

Another way to block pinholes in your screen is to just use masking tape or scotch tape. This method should only be used if you are printing less than about 500 t-shirts because after a while ink can ooze through the bottom of the tape and get on to your t-shirts. You will want to tape off the inside of your screens to allow for easy ink clean up after you are done printing. To do this, use two-inch masking tape (or wider tape if you have any) and put down layers onto the screen on all four sides of the frame. Keep laying down tape slightly overlapping the last strip you put down until you reach the emulsion. Make sure that the corners where the fabric meets the frame of the screen are covered by tape so that ink will not be able to seep into the cracks. This will make cleaning up the ink much easier.

Exercise

If you have not already, watch the video on how to silkscreen it should have come with your basic supply kit. Then take the first piece of artwork that came in the basic supply kit and practice burning your first screen with this. If it does not work wash out the screen and do it again until it works.

Chapter 4

–

Artwork

Artwork is the starting point of screen-printing. The first step to a final printed t-shirt is obtaining or making the artwork of the desired print. This chapter explains the methods for preparing artwork to be burned onto a silkscreen and how to burn a silk-screen.

Color Separation

Art for screen-printing can be pretty much anything you want to put on a t-shirt, but before you can get anything on a t-shirt it must be color separated. Color separation is taking each individual color in the selected piece of artwork and separating it on separate pieces of paper.

For example, printing the numbers 1234 on a t-shirt, each being different colors, "1" is red, "2" is blue, "3" is purple, and "4" is green. In order to accomplish this each number is printed on separate pieces of paper. One paper with "1" on it printed in black, one with "2" on it printed in black, one with "3" on it printed in black, and the last with "4" on it printed in black.

Below is an example of this color separation.

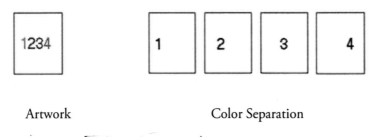

Artwork   Color Separation

Each of the above color separations gets burned onto a separate screen, which holds and prints the appropriate color of ink. You need one screen for every color you print. You can switch colors of your t-shirt print with just a few minutes time by simply switching the color of ink in your burned screen.

For a one-color print there is no need to color separate. If your original artwork is in multiple colors and you would like to print it out in one color, then just print a black and white copy of the artwork. Then you will be able to burn a screen and print in any color you want.

Four-Color Process

Four-Color Process is a method of using halftones and four screens with black, cyan, magenta, and yellow in them to print hundreds of colors. Four-Color Process is the way that screen-printers are able to print photographic images onto t-shirts. Due to the level of experience needed to print good four-color process t-shirts we do not explain all the intricacies of it in this manual. After a few months of printing, one is usually experienced enough to start learning to do four-color processes.

Final Artwork Preparations

Before you can burn an image onto a silk-screen your artwork (each color separation if it is more than one color) must be on either clear paper (over-head projection paper) or vellum (which is see through but slightly foggy). You can go to your local copy shop and have a clear positive made of your color separations. Using overhead projection paper it is good to have two copies of each color separation made so that you can tape them together to double the ability for the clear positive to stop light from passing through the printed portion. You may also print directly onto vellum with a laser printer if your artwork is on a computer. Because vellum is not clear, doubling up two of the same print to darken the image does not help as it also stops the light from passing through the rest of the paper. To darken the image printed on vellum you can use artist's fixative (also called toner), which you can get at some screen printing supply stores or art supply stores. Make sure the fixative you get does not have any UV (ultra violet) block. Passing the artwork through the laser printer a second time can help darken it as well. Make certain any toner-saving modes are disabled when printing your artwork.

Once your artwork has each of its colors on a separate piece of vellum or a separate clear positive, you are ready for the next step – Burning a screen!

How to do Color Separations in Adobe Photoshop

Step 1. Import your artwork

Open Adobe Photoshop. Upon Startup you will have a blank screen. Open your artwork by using the "file" tab then the "open..." selection.

File/Open... Example: ▶

A new dialogue box opens like this: ▶

Select the file and click the open button to open the file in Adobe Photoshop. Photoshop allows you to preview the files before you open them. It also notes the file size underneath. You will now see your artwork in Adobe Photoshop.

Step 2. Separate your colors.

Now you can start separating your colors. The first thing is to select each color one by one. I will start by selecting the red **C**. To do this, go to:

Select/Color Range... Example ▶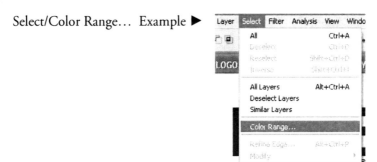

You will see a dialogue box that looks like ▼

When you turn up the fuzziness, the amount of variation of color selected increases. Turning down the fuzziness selects a smaller range of similar colors, i.e. pink and light pink instead of pink, light pink, very light pink, and dark pink. In order to select the color you want, move the Color Range Dialogue Box away from the intended color to select. Notice that when the Color Range Dialogue Box is open, the pointer over your image is now in the shape of the eyedropper tool. The eyedropper tool simply represents that when you click a color, that color will be selected. Move the eyedropper tool (your mouse curser) over the color you want to select. In the simple image I am selecting red. Click on the color. That color will now be selected when you press the okay button.

To help you see more clearly what color you selected use the Selection Preview pull down menu and select Grayscale.

Notice that after you select Grayscale every color that is not selected turns black on your main image. This quickly shows you what color you have selected. It may be easier to select the colors you want in the smaller version of your image that is located inside the Color Range dialogue box. Notice that I have also turned the fuzziness up to 150 this is because I want to capture as much of the red as I can. In my image the outside of my Red "**C**" starts to turn slightly pink at the edge. In order to make sure that I get that pinkish edge, I turn the fuzziness up to 150. When I turn the Fuzziness past 150 I start to also select parts of the black "**H B**".

When I have Grayscale selected and I select the red "**C**" this is what it looks like:

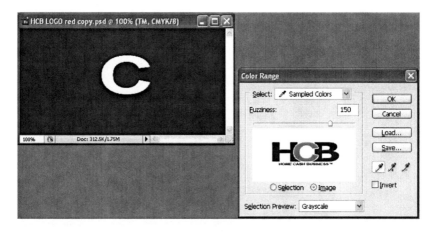

Every color not selected appears as black. Now that I have the color I want selected, I press ok and the Color Range dialogue box disappears.

If you look closely the "**C**" is outlined showing you that all the red color in the "**C**" has been selected.

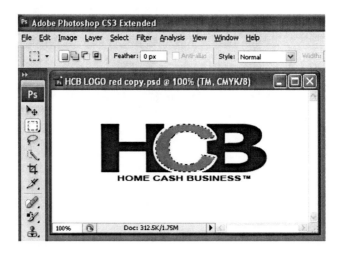

Here is a close up on the "**C**" illustrating the outline:

E CASH BUSINE

    Notice the outline does not cover the entire area that encloses the "**C**." A tiny bit of light red was not selected. This is because the fuzziness was set too low. Try increasing the fuzziness on your image until you get all of the color that you need selected. Sometimes you will not be able to get all of the color that you want. This creates problems because when you copy the color over to its own layer you are copying a smaller image than the one that is shown on the screen. This will make registration impossible most of the time. We will show you how to correct this later simply by enlarging (stroking) the layer.

    The next step in separating the color will be to turn it solid black for the printing purposes. Remember to print all the colors black in order to get a good burn on the screen. After you burn the screen you will be able to use any color you want. Now that the "**C**" is selected – we know it is selected by the outline – we can change it to black by clicking the "Edit" tab and selecting the "Fill..." option.

    Edit/Fill... Example ▶

The dialogue box looks like ▶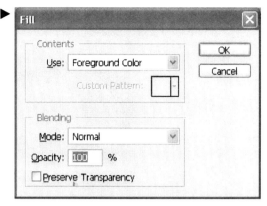

Use the Contents pull down menu and select the Black option.

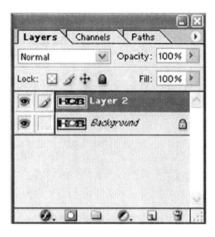

➤ Now that black is selected, press the ok button. The result is a very dark black "**C**." Note that the "**C**" is still selected. Instead of being red, it is dark black. This is what we want, but we need to print it separately from the "**H B**" so we put it in its own layer. Look at the Layers window pictured to the right. This toolbox is usually open when you start Photoshop. If you do not see this window you can open it by going to the "Windows" tab and selecting the "Layers" option.

There are two layers there now. One with the original image and the second layer, which is the original image with the "**C**" turned black. Photoshop automatically created a new layer when we turned the "**C**" black so that we do not corrupt the original image. Because Photoshop adds layers over the original layer, you can revert back to your original image at any time by simply deleting the other layers and leaving the layer labeled "Background."

We want to create a layer with a black "**C**" only. This is relatively simple, because the black "**C**" is still selected on the main image. Press the "Crtl" Button on the keyboard and simultaneously press the "c" button. In other words Ctrl + C. This will copy the "**C**" into the computers memory (Or whatever is currently selected (outlined) on your image.) Then you want to "Paste" it into the layers window. Select the Layers Window by clicking with the mouse pointer on the top edge of the window (the blue part) or by clicking inside the window below the other layers in the blank grey space. After the Layers Window is selected you can press Ctrl + V that is the Crtl button and the "v" button simultaneously. When that is done the "**C**" will appear in a layer all by itself.

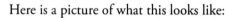

Here is a picture of what this looks like:

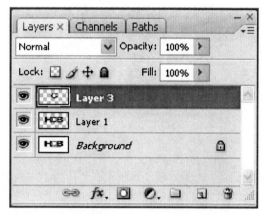

Right now the "**C**" layer is selected. You can tell by the fact that it is highlighted blue. Before selecting and separating your other colors make sure to select the "Background" layer first.

The next thing we want to do is select the "**H B**" and put them into their own layer. Follow the same procedure as putting the "**C**" into its own layer. Here is a quick recap on how to do this.

1. Select the "Background" Layer
2. Go to Select/Color Range…
3. Click on desired color
4. Adjust the Fuzziness if needed, press OK
5. Go to Edit/Fill…
6. Select Use: Black, Press OK
7. Press Ctrl + "c" to copy
8. Select Layers Window
9. Press Ctrl + "v" to paste

Refer to the above 9 easy steps to separate all of the colors on your image. Here is what my Layers Window looks like when I am finished:

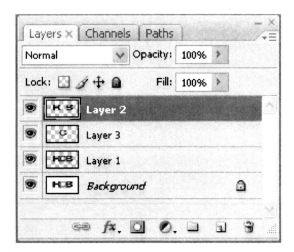

Step 3. Manipulate your Art to Make the Printing Easy.

One thing that can make the difference between having a horrible time of getting a print to register and having a wonderful, easy time of getting a print to register is something called Trapping. Trapping is a process in which you make one or more of your colors slightly larger than it was originally in order to make registration easier.

Here is a simplified example below.

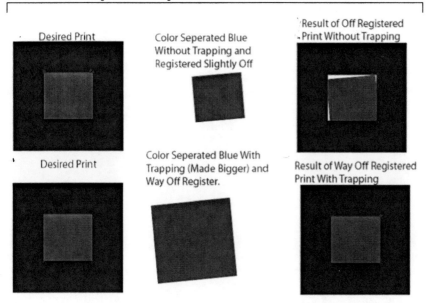

Notice that if we make the blue square bigger, print it, then print the black over it, it covers up the unwanted blue. We are left with a perfect looking print that can very easily be re-registered whenever needed. Now that we see the benefits of trapping lets learn how to do it Photoshop. Before you do any trapping it is important to remember that when screen printing, the darker colors always cover the lighter colors, and so they will be printed last. Usually in this order: white, yellow, red, blue, black. So always do your trapping with this in mind.

In a lot of prints there is a black outline around the whole thing. Trapping would be easy for this because your can just adjust the black a little bit and leave the other colors alone. Here is how it is done. Double click on the layer you want to adjust to allow for trapping (make bigger). A Layer Style dialogue box will pop up that looks like this ▼

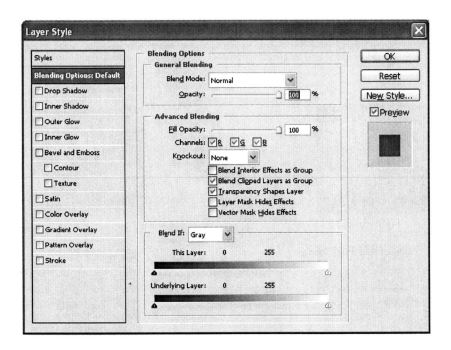

You can ignore everything else except the check box in the bottom left corner that says "Stroke." Check the box, and click the rectangle around the word "Stroke." This will highlight it and the dialogue box will then look like the one pictured on the next page.

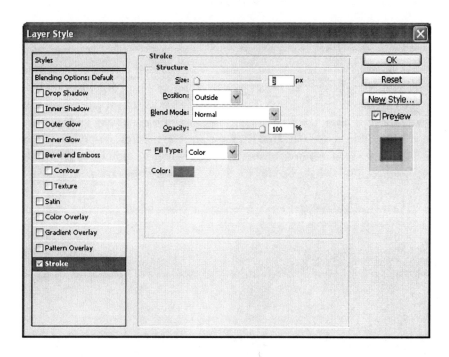

Take a look at your main image after you check the stroke box. You will notice that it has a thin outline around the layer you have selected. Stroke just means outline. The outline may be a different color than black. You will want to change the outline color to black. You do that by clicking on the color box located in the middle of the dialogue box, and then selecting black as the stroke color. You can control the size (width) of the outline by adjusting the arrow to the right of the word "Size" located in the top center of the dialogue box, or by simply typing in the amount of pixels thick you would like your outline to be.

I set my color to black and decided I wanted to make the letters of my image a little thicker so they'd be easier to read and easier to point. So I stroked the "H B" with a 3 pixel thick outline. Then I pressed ok to save changes and get rid of the dialogue box.

Step 4. Print the artwork.

In order to print your artwork you have to make it so only the layer you want printed is showing on the screen. To do this, we turn our attention back to the Layers window. The little eyes located to the left of the layer name designate that the layer is visible. By clicking the little eye of any layer you can turn it invisible or *hide* it. This is important for printing purposes. On the previous page is an example of the "**C**" layer being the only layer left visible. Notice that the eyes have been clicked off the other three layers.

Below is what my main image looks like when I hide the other layers.

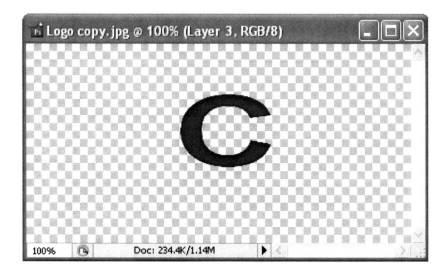

When you see only one of the colors that you want to print left on the screen, you are ready to print.

Go to File/Print with Preview… You will get this screen:

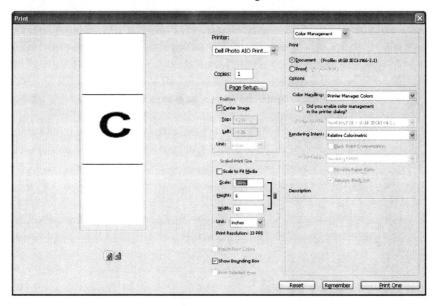

In this dialogue box it gives us the option to choose the size we would like our image to be. You can input the height or width in inches or just simply scale it until it looks the right size when it's printed onto the page. If you want to adjust the orientation that the image is printed on the page, press the Page Setup… button. This will allow you to print the image out in the landscape mode (sideways on the paper).

Once your image is the proper orientation and scaled correctly press the Print button. Remember to make absolute sure that you scale all the images by the exact same amount. Scaling the different colors of your image differently will make them impossible to register most of the time. Repeat the steps involved in printing until all your separated colors are printed.

Here's a quick recap on how to print each color.

1. Click off the eyes in the Layers Window on every color but one.
2. Go to File/Print With Preview…
3. Scale the Image.
4. If necessary print the image sideways on the page by selecting Landscape.
5. Press Print.

Chapter 5

-

Inks

The leading type of ink for printing t-shirts is plastisol ink because of how easy it makes printing. Plastisol ink is thick, durable and does not dry up in your screen. The drawbacks of plastisol are that you can not dry clean it or iron over it. (You can turn clothes inside out and iron them if they are printed though).

Plastisol Ink Types

All-purpose ink is the general ink you will use while printing t-shirts. These come in a very wide range of colors. They are ideal for printing over underbases and on light t-shirts.

High opacity (HO) inks are inks used to cover dark t-shirts and material. When an ink is high opacity it just means that it will cover better with less ink.

Low bleed refers to plastisol ink that is resistant to allowing polyester dyes to seep through them. When polyester shirts are printed after a few days the color will start to be absorbed into the ink. This is especially apparent in white ink on dark shirts. Low bleed ink will prevent this from happening and should be used when printing on polyester or partially polyester shirts.

Flash cure white ink is ink that can be flash dried in a few seconds with a flash dryer. This ink is primarily used to print underbases. A white underbase on dark shirt is used to make the color you print over it show up much brighter. Four color process inks come in black, cyan, magenta, and yellow. They are used for four-color process printing. Four-color process printing is where you just use four colors to print realistic images on t-shirts. There are also athletic plastisol inks. These are more duable and thicker than regular plastisol.

Curing Plastisol

In order for plastisol ink to dry it must be brought up to about 280-320° F. This is usually done with a conveyer dryer by placing the t-shirt on the conveyer belt and letting pass through the dryer. Most conveyer dryers dry a t-shirt in under a minute. However, when people are just starting out they sometimes just use a flash dryer to fully cure their t-shirts. This is done by placing the t-shirt on a table or stool, turning the flash dryer over the shirt, and leaving it for about 45 seconds to a minute.

To test the t-shirt to see if it is fully cured, you can use a stretch test. This is done by grabbing the printed portion of the shirt and pinching it with your index and thumb with both your hands and stretching the ink apart. If you notice the ink crack or separate this means that the ink is not fully cured. Run the shirt through the conveyer dryer again or put it back under the flash dryer until the ink no longer breaks apart when stretched. If the ink is not fully cured it will fade and will be likely to wash out when the garment is washed. The most definitive test to see if the ink is fully cured is to actually wash the t-shirt. If the ink comes off during the wash then you will need to make sure you dry the rest of the t-shirts more thoroughly.

When using a conveyer dryer you will notice that the speed of the conveyer belt and the heat of the heat panels will be adjustable. If you turn the heat panels up all the way it will probably scorch the t-shirt, if you turn the speed of the conveyer belt all the way up the ink probably wont dry. It is a good idea to experiment until you find a good conveyer belt pace and heat temperature to fit your printing speed and that fully cures the t-shirt. You will notice that with lower heat temperatures you will have more leeway to adjust belt speed between under curing and scorching your t-shirts. To start move the elements as high as possible, raise the temperature to the maximum and adjust the speed of the belt until the ink dries well.

Mixing Inks

You can mix inks to get the desired color you want. This process is much like mixing paint. Make sure to use a lot less of the darker ink when mixing two inks. You should also remember that when you buy ink it will generally be a brighter color then when you mix inks to get the same color. Ask your ink supplier about ink systems specially designed for mixing.

Water Based Inks

Water based inks are tough to work with because they will dry up in your screen. Sometimes the ink will dry up in the screen and you will be unable to wash it out. To prevent the ink from drying in the screen you have to do a flood stroke (this is described later in the Printing Chapter). There are also retarder additives that you can mix into the ink that slow the drying process. Because of how fast water based inks dry, when you start printing you will have to keep printing for the entire job. Even leaving the screen idle for a couple minutes will usually let water based inks dry up in your screen. When this happens you will have to wipe all the ink out of the image on your screen. The reason people use water based ink is because it is very thin and absorbs into the fabric of whatever it is you're printing it on. Water based ink is very popular to use on beach towels. You can also iron and dry clean water based prints so they are used on fashion clothing. With the use of a catalyst you can simply print water based ink and let them air dry on cloths lines. Other methods are to use heat lamps, flash dryers with a fan blowing underneath or ironing the print with a sheet of heat transfer paper over the print.

Exercise

Call one or two of the supply places in the back of the book and get a catalogue for inks.

Chapter 6
—
Printing

We are finally ready to print!

Set Up

The set up differs slightly for the type of equipment you get. Generally you place the screens in the clamps of your printing press, register the colors, add the ink, and put in the squeegees, and print. The first thing to do is to put the screens on the printing press. The printing press will have "arms" with clamps at the end of it to clamp the screen in. Every arm a printing press has allows you to print one color. When putting your screens on your printing press arrange them so that the lightest colors go first. Generally this means you will order them white, yellow, then orange, green etc., then red, blue, purple etc. and always lastly print black. All you need to remember is that darker colors are printed last. This will make sure that any registration traps (overlapping inks) are covered properly. You might want to do any taping of the edges of the screen while it is on the press rather than right after you apply screen block to it. This is because the press does a nice job of holding the screen steady.

Aligning Your Print

The second step is to align your screen so that when you pull the screen down it lines up straight with the shirtboard. This will insure that every shirt gets a level print. To do this you take a black marker and a straight edge and draw a line down the center of the shirtboard. Then take the screen and bring it down on the shirt board (pull the arm down with the screen in it). You will be able to see the marker line behind the screen. Just align the image on the screen so that it is center with the line and also if the image has any horizontal lines make sure they are square with the line. After you do this tighten down the printer knobs to lock the screen in place. If you have a multi color job just align one screen (usually your black ink screen as it is the one you will align your other colors to). If you are only doing a one color then you are done. If your screen is already taped, then all you need to do is add ink, select the appropriate squeegee and start printing.

Registering Multicolor Prints

One way to align the multi colors is to take a print of the finished image or you can use the color separations, tape it to the shirtboard and align the screens to that. Alternately, after you have one of your screens aligned then you can register the other colors off it. To do this you simply print a test square with your aligned color. Remember to spray glue the shirtboard before placing the test square down. Flash cure the test square. Now take your other screens and put them down over the printed test square, loosen the knobs holding the screen in place and adjust the screen until it is lined up with the color printed on your test square. Repeat for any additional colors.

The next thing to do before printing an actual t-shirt is to fully print a test square to make sure the print is fully registered and no ink is getting onto the garment through pinholes. Simply fill the screens with the desired colors. Lay squeegees in the screens that are slightly larger than the print. Over sized squeegees work fine if that is all you have. Then print the various colors onto the test square. If a color is not aligned properly flash cure the test square again. Squeegee all the ink in the unaligned screen down into the bottom of it. Use a rag and some mineral spirits or soy solvent (or any ink cleaner) to clean the ink out of the fabric. This is done so you can see through the screen, because after you print with a screen you usually cannot see through it well enough to register it again. Reregister the screen and do another test print.

Test squares are available at screen-printing supply stores by the hundreds. You can also print on newsprint type paper towels. These are the type found in commercial bathrooms and can be purchased at any cleaning supply store. Remember that if you are printing on dark t-shirts you will need to either print a white underbase or print a color, flash cure it, and print it again sometimes to get a nice solid color down. When flash curing it is important that you do not cure the ink all the way. You know you have flash cured correctly when the ink is still tacky to the touch but does not come off on your finger.

Squeegees and Squeegeeing

There are different squeegees and squeegeeing techniques that accomplish different ends. Squeegees with slightly rounded edges force more ink through the screen. These are usually used when printing light colors on dark shirts to help the ink completely cover the shirt. Sharp edged squeegees allow less ink to pass through. Sharp edged squeegees are good for really fine lined printing.

Soft rubbered squeegees are good for people who like to pull the ink through the screen rather than push it. They also force more ink through. Harder rubbered squeegees do not force as much ink through the screen, and can give a crisper print when it is needed. Sometimes you will want to use a hard squeegee and squeegee the print two or three times to get a lot of ink down and maintain a sharp print.

Squeegeeing is the action of passing the squeegee over the screen and forcing the ink down through the screen onto the shirt. You can either drag a puddle of ink across the screen toward you and press it back hard away from you or just pull hard while pressing down and make the print as the squeegee comes toward you. Either way works. It is important to note that pull printing will bring the image about 1/16th of an inch higher than when you push print. Because of this fact you can only squeegee one way with a particular screen after you do the first stroke. You can use this to your advantage if the screen is slightly off register. If the register of a color is too low than you can try pull squeegeeing rather than push squeegeeing and it might raise the register high enough to put the color back on register.

Flood Stroke

A flood stroke is used when you are working with inks that dry up on your screen, or when you are flash drying plastisol inks on your shirtboard and it causes the ink to dry up on your screen (from printing on a hot shirtboard). To do a flood stroke just collect a portion of the ink and pull an even coat of ink over the screen without pressing any ink through. As you pull the squeegee back let a thin film of ink slide underneath it and cover the screen. Let the ink sit there as you squeegee the other colors or switch the t-shirt, and when you print the color that was flood stroked just press the ink that you left covering the ink through. Then do another flood stroke and leave a thin film of ink covering the screen again.

Flood strokes prevent the ink from drying in the image of the screen by leaving a relatively thick layer of ink over the image on the screen. This makes it take longer for any ink to dry up in the image because there is plenty of wet ink over the image stopping any of the ink from drying up.

Getting a Rhythm Down

After your print is registered, your dryer is turned on and heated up, you are ready to start really cranking out the printed t-shirts. Here are some good tricks to help you get a rhythm going and help you get the job done faster. Make sure the printer is right next to your conveyer dryer. You should

36

not have to take a step to get your t-shirts from the shirtboard to the conveyer belt. The shirtboard should be on one side of you and the conveyer belt should be on the other side of you.

If you are drying shirts with a flash cure unit then it is a good idea to be printing one shirt while another shirt is drying. It is a good idea to have a timer set for about 45 - 60 seconds to prevent you from scorching shirts. You can stream line the putting of shirts onto the shirtboard by taking them out of the box unfolding them and laying them flat on a stool or table next to your printing press. If you are printing the front of the shirt then lay them back side up and grab them by the opening on the bottom with both hands thumbs down. When you go to put the shirt on the shirtboard the front will be the side that is on top of the shirtboard. If you're printing the back then lay them front side up. On an order of a couple hundred shirts this can shave 30 minutes off the printing time doing this.

Every 3 – 12 shirts you print you will need to spray more spray adhesive onto your shirtboard to make sure the t-shirt stays in place. You will know when you need more if a shirt partially comes up off the board when you're lifting the screen up. After the first dozen or so shirts you will probably have a nice rhythm going and you will love counting the money add up as you are making from $2 - $10 dollars a minute printing the shirts. However after about 50 – 100 shirts or so you will probably start to run out of ink in your screens. When this happens just go ahead and add more and then go back to adding the money up in your head – err I mean printing.

As a printer you will probably get some ink on some t-shirts from your hands from time to time. They have what is called a blowout gun or spotgun that removes small spots of ink from t-shirts. It will prove to be a good investment to have one of these things around as fingerprints and other small ink marks will over time add up to lost money. To blow ink out with a blowout gun you need to fully cure the ink spot and then use the gun. Trying to blowout wet ink just spreads the ink all over the t-shirt. After all the shirts are printed, sort them into dozens and fold them in half and stick them in the box they came in. Make sure to sort them by size. And now they are ready to be picked up or delivered.

Cleaning Up

After the printing is done you will need to clean the ink out of the screens. To do this, lay down a newspaper sheet on the shirtboard and then put the screen down on top of it and use the squeegee to force all the ink down to the bottom of the screen. Then take the squeegee and scrape the excess ink on it back into your ink container. Then take the rest of the ink in the screen and put it back into your ink container (plastic putty knives are ideal for this).

Now lift the tape that is around the edges of your screen and throw it away. There should be just a thin film of ink left in the screen. Take two rags (cotton rags work best) and some ink cleaner (soy solvent or mineral spirits) and wash away the film. Get any ink that may have gotten on the rest of the screen. Repeat for the rest of the screens. Also use some ink cleaner and rags to clean the squeegees. Put the ink away and you are all done!

Reclaiming Screens

Reclaiming a screen means to take all the emulsion off the screen so you can burn another image onto it. With a lot of prints the customer may want to do more shirts at a later date, so you will want to store the screens so that you can use them later. But sometimes the print your doing is only for doing a one time print, so you will want to reclaim the screens so you can use them for another print later.

Reclaiming the screen must be done away from ultraviolet light similar to when burning the screen. Use a rag to rub reclaimer onto the emulsion of the screen. Rub it on both sides and wait for about 1 ½ to 2 minutes and then wash it off with a **pressure washer**. The pressure washing can be done outside in the shade, but must happen within 2 minutes of applying the reclaimer. All the emulsion should wash off. If some emulsion is left just repeat the process until all the emulsion is gone. Expect to see a ghost of the image you just printed still left on the screen. This is normal, but sometimes you will have actual ink clogging the holes of the fabric. Try using ink cleaner to get it out, but in some instances this will not work and you will need to use haze remover. Haze remover is made specifically for this purpose. Follow the directions on the can for best results. To minimize the need to use haze remover try to clean the screen as best you can directly after you finish printing. After the screen is reclaimed just degrease it and it will be ready to be coated again.

Exercise

Buy any screen printing package (1 through 6) and use the art work or screen you have already burned or the new artwork or screen you made and set it up and print on your first t-shirt or test paper. Now you are officially a silkscreener and you have the equipment and supplies to start marketing and selling your service.

Chapter 7
–
Sales

The best advertising money you can spend is joining the local Chamber of Commerce; if you join and go to all their luncheons and benefits you will have more orders than you know what to do with. I can not tell you how many people have told me that. The most important part of any business big or small is sales and the number one reason they fail is the lack of basic sales skills. I can tell you that if you follow these basic policies you can survive, and if you keep on improving your ability to sell you will make a fortune.

Define your product - know what it is backward and forward. If you have to get some modeling clay and actually make a model of what your product is and how it comes about then do it. The number one problem with business is no one knows what product they produce. If asked most people think they make money (unless they work for the US mint then that is not what they actually make). If an individual simply figured out what they produced at work they would live a much happier life. So know what you produce, then produce more of it.

In other words for t-shirt printing you do not just produce "t-shirts". You can get more specific than this and it will help you in the way that you go after customers and at every point of making your business grow. You could get a little more specific and say "printed t-shirts," or even better "superior quality printed t-shirts that make the customers feel that they have gotten an excellent exchange for their money."

Next, if you have a product, then have a good price on it where you can make a profit and pay the bills. Also, work out the exchange with the public, and give the customer a high quality product for a good price. Doing these three things, you will never have to worry about surviving as a company. The best policy to have once you have defined your product and pricing is this,

"DELIVER WHAT YOU PROMISE"

If you tell someone you will have it done at a certain time have it done no matter what! I do not care what you have to do, and that means stay up all night if you have to.

This does not mean tell them in 4 weeks it will be done, because the next important thing is this,

"Speed of particle flow determines power"

Basically, if you get orders and get them out flawlessly and fast you will become a powerful company that exchanges with the public and that means prosperity for you and your employees and all the families involved.

Promotion

I have heard of several ways to get t-shirt orders from my customers over the years that I would like to share with you. The first was from a phone salesman who simply started with the A's in the yellow pages and called and got leads to follow up and procure orders. He made a comment that t-shirt selling was the easiest thing for him to sell. The next is to just let everyone you know, friends, business acquaintances, and people you have daily contact with (video store, super market) that you now print t-shirts. The rule when starting any new business is to make your business known.

Here are just a few ways to get your services known:

- Business cards
- Flyers
- Tell your friends and acquaintances
- Talk to schools, clubs, organizations, businesses, churches, chamber of commerce and much, much more.
- Newspaper ads

Remember the best way to advertise is to reach as many people as possible without spending large amounts of money. The great thing about t-shirts is that it is a great advertising vehicle, for all kinds of organizations. Below is a list of who you can contact for further books on sales.

A Great Book and a Little Inspirational Pep Talk

A great book to read is "Rich Dad, Poor Dad" by Robert Kiyosaki. Visit his website at, www.richdad.com. This book will teach you that being rich is an attitude not just being lucky and having a lot of money. It will teach how to gain that attitude and become rich. There is also an important book to read on sales called "Sales Dogs" this book is a comprehensive guide on how to sell using your special skills as a person not by barking down someone's throat. This book can also be found on richdad.com.

Afterword

One of the big lessons in life you will no doubt run into the minute you say I want to survive (or I want to make the biggest business or sing or whatever goals you have), is the friend who says you cannot. There can be people in your environment who simply do not want you to make it for what ever reason in their minds - good or bad. Do not let these people influence you. It will slow you down at best and can make you sick and depressed at worst. If you have a dream - follow it. When the people who say it cannot be done are right we are all worse off, so do a good deed for everyone and make them wrong. The world will be that much better because of it.

We wish you all the success and if there is anything we can help you with please email anytime tshirt@homecashbusiness.com or call (800) 311-8962 or write to:

HCB
PO Box 2270
Smithfield, NC 27577

Thank you for purchasing our products

- The HCB production and technical team.

Appendix A - Equipment

Package 1

Six-Color Silkscreen Machine, 16" x 16" Flash Dryer, Exposure Unit, Tools, Supplies, and Training Video and Manual

Newly created to handle the demand for a low cost start up kit that could do everything the BIG stuff did but without the initial high start-up investment. Take it from me; I've been building silkscreen equipment for over 17 years now and when I developed this kit I made it so the colors register just as well as larger setups I build. I found out from all the e-mails I receive on a daily basis that you want to start up your own home business but you can not afford the initial large cash outlay you need to get started. WELL HERE IT IS!!! Everything you need to start printing t-shirts professionally at Home RIGHT NOW!! You can print t-shirts, sweatshirts, and stickers too!

THE AMAZING MULTI-COLOR SILKSCREEN KIT INCLUDES:

E-Z TECH SIX-COLOR TABLETOP TEXTILE PRINTER: made with portable durable steel powder coated to resist rust and chemical erosion. Easy to carry anywhere, fairs, events, family reunions etc. Capable of printing 60 shirts an hour.

6 - PAIRS of E-Z TECH Multi-Color Registration Brackets. For each color you want to print on a t-shirt a silkscreen is required and it must be in registration so every time you lay a silkscreen down on the shirt it lines up in the exact same place. These brackets easily attach to a silkscreen so you can properly register each color. They are made from steel anodized to resist rust and chemical erosion. There are enough brackets for 6 silk-screens. Additional brackets are available.

E-Z TECH 16 x 16 FLASH DRYER operates on 110 volts 15amps of electricity and is powder coated to resist rust and chemical erosion. 1 year warranty on the heating element. A flash dryer is essential to the drying process for plastisol ink needed to do a professional job. When the ink is dried properly (1 minute at 6 inches away) this ink will not wash out like iron on or heat transfers.

E-Z TECH EXPOSURE LIGHT Steel construction and powder coated 500 watt halogen light used for putting the image into the silkscreen.

BASIC SUPPLY KIT described below.

Upgrade Path
If your customer base builds up to where you need to do a much larger volume faster check this out---> Buy this kit and when you decide to purchase package # 2 or # 3 take $500 off the price!!! See other packages for details.

Statistics on the
SIX-COLOR SILKSCREEN MACHINE

I just finished printing on the amazing multi-color silkscreen machine for my first time and here are the results: I printed 24 white t-shirts 100% heavy weight cotton with my three color logo yellow, green and black. The logo was an 11" design and placed on the back of the t-shirt. I paid a graphic artist $50 for the design. He separated the colors and gave me the three positives needed to burn the screens. This artist and others are available for you to use for your home cash business if you cannot find an artist in your area. If you are not an artist it is best that you pay someone to do the work. You will save yourself a lot of headaches in the end. When you take on a job the artwork is always charged extra and is not part of the pricing in printing t-shirts for someone.

Labor Time:

10 minutes to coat the screen with emulsion:

15 minutes to burn the image into the screen

30 minutes to wash the image

30 minutes to set up the screens and register the print

52 minutes to print a three color print onto 24 t-shirts

137 minutes to do the whole job from start to finish or 2 hours and 17 minutes

Material Costs:

- $0.73 Silkscreen costs (A silkscreen costs $20.00 but can be used up to 5,000 times changing images as many times as you need.)
- $1.50 Emulsion (coating you put on a screen in order to burn the image in the screen)
- $0.50 Plastic tape
- $2.70 Ink (note; it cost .035 per imprint per color)
- $44.00 T-shirt cost ($22.00/dozen for 100% cotton 6.0oz t-shirt)
- $0.20 Electricity - I called to get the actual cost per hour to run the flash dyer.

$49.62 Total cost of material to print the above t-shirts

Normal charge for 24 white t-shirts would be $8.00 each. Remember, artwork is a separate charge and is extra profit if you do the artwork yourself. $192.00 would be the price charged.

$ 49.62 material costs.

$142.38 PROFIT LEFT AFTER MATERIAL COSTS

Total Labor hours are 2 hours and 17 minutes, which works out to $62.35 per HOUR!

Package 2
Six-Color One-Station Rotary Printer, 16" x 16" Flash Dryer, Exposure Unit, Tools, Supplies, and Training Video and Manual

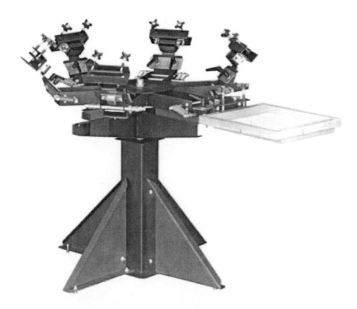

E-Z TECH Six-Color One-Station Textile Printer
- 27" maximum screen width with six screens
- One 16" x 18" platen
- Print 240 one-color shirts per hour (with conveyor dryer)
- Produces professional quality prints
- All durable steel construction
- Powder coated to resist rust and chemical erosion
- Adjustable Handles for Easy Registration
- Heavy duty 4 spring tension system to handle any type of attachment
- 3ft x 11in turning radius with 24in x 24in screens.
- Recommended minimum 10ft x 10ft area for printing
- Tilt adjustment
- Modular design transforms into a 6-color 4-station when you are ready
- 3 year limited warranty
- Made in the USA

E-Z TECH Flash Dryer

- 1800 watts of heat
- high quality molded ceramic infrared heating element
- 120v, 15amps of electricity
- Height adjustable 26" to 52"
- Cures 60 shirts per hour
- Free standing unit
- 8ft heavy duty cord
- On/off switch
- Powder coated finish
- Durable all steel construction
- 1 year limited warranty
- Made in the USA

E-Z TECH Exposure Light
- 500 watt halogen light
- Durable steel construction
- Powder coated finish
- Extra bulb
- Professional burns
- 1 year limited warranty

Package 3
Six-Color Four-Station Rotary Printer, 16" x 16" Flash Dryer, Exposure Unit, Tools, Supplies, and Training Video and Manual

E-Z TECH Six-Color Four-Station Textile Printer
- 27" maximum screen width with six screens
- Four 16" x 18" platens
- Print 300 one-color shirts per hour (with conveyor dryer)
- Produces professional quality prints
- All durable steel construction
- Powder coated to resist rust and chemical erosion
- Adjustable Handles for Easy Registration
- Heavy duty 4 spring tension system to handle any type of attachment
- 3ft x 11in turning radius with 24in x 24in screens.
- Recommended minimum 10ft x 10ft area for printing
- Tilt adjustment
- Modular design transforms into a 6-color 4-station when you are ready
- 3 year limited warranty
- Made in the USA

E-Z TECH Flash Dryer

- 1800 watts of heat
- high quality molded ceramic infrared heating element
- 120v, 15amps of electricity
- Heigh adjustable 26" to 52"
- Cures 60 shirts per hour
- Free standing unit
- 8ft heavy duty cord
- On/off switch
- Powder coated finish
- Durable all steel construction
- 1 year limited warranty
- Made in the USA

E-Z TECH Exposure Light
- 500 watt halogen light
- Durable steel construction
- Powder coated finish
- Extra bulb
- Professional burns
- 1 year limited warranty

Maxi Conveyor

Maxi Conveyor Features:

- 4800 total watts of heat using two 2400 watt elements.
- high quality molded ceramic infrared heating elements.
- 230v, 22amp of electricity.
- 24in x 24in heating area.
- 8ft long with a 24in wide belt.
- Variable speed motor.
- Separate temperature control for each element.
- Separate height adjustment for each element.
- Dry t-shirts the easy way up to 300 shirts per hour.
- 8ft heavy duty Cord.
- Powder coated finish.
- 1 year limited warranty.
- Made in the USA.

Mini Conveyor

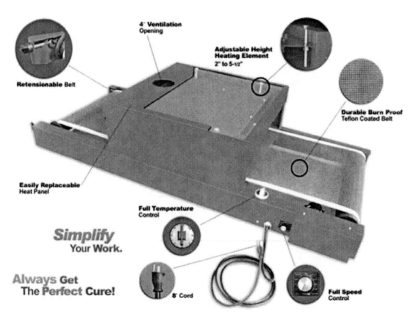

4" Ventilation Opening

Adjustable Height Heating Element 2" to 5-½"

Retensionable Belt

Durable Burn Proof Teflon Coated Belt

Easily Replaceable Heat Panel

Full Temperature Control

Simplify
Your Work.

Always Get
The Perfect Cure!

8' Cord

Full Speed Control

SPEED UP YOUR PRODUCTION - ORDER YOURS TODAY!

Mini Conveyor Features:
- 2400 watts of heat.
- high quality molded ceramic infrared heating element
- 120v, 20amp of electricity
- 120 volt just plug in any 120 wall socket with 20amp breaker.
- 18in x 18in heating area.
- No assembly required.
- 5ft long with a 20in wide belt.
- Variable speed motor.
- Temperature control.
- Height adjustable heat panel.
- Dry t-shirts the easy way up to 120 shirts per hour.
- 8ft heavy duty Cord
- Powder coated finish
- 1 year limited warranty
- Made in the USA

Basic Supply Kit
Included with equipment packages 1 - 6

SUPPLIES INCLUDED:

- 16 OZ EMULSION
- 16 OZ DEGREASER
- 16 OZ RECLAIMER
- 16 OZ SOY SOLVENT
- 16 OZ BLACK PLASTISOL INK
- 8 OZ SCREEN BLOCK
- CAN OF SPRAY ADHESIVE
- 1 ROLL OF TAPE
- 10 TEST PELLONS
- 20 SHEETS OF VELLUM

TOOLS INCLUDED:

- 1 SILKSCREEN 21" X 19"
- 1 SQUEEGEE 14"
- 1 SCREEN COATER 14"
- TRAINING VIDEO & MANUAL

Success Stories
Here is an e-mail from a happy customer!

May 13, 2000
Bob:
Just wanted to drop you a line to let you know that every thing you said about your equipment was true. (As you well know!) We purchased package number one with the other materials offered. The first week we had four orders. One for a ball team (32 shirts). The second order was for a banner for the local primary school. The third order was for t-shirts for a relay team (24 shirts). The fourth is for our bible school at our local church. We have not screened the fourth order because they are not due till July. Bob, I have said all of this for two reasons. One is that with a minor investment we were able to supplement our income in a major way. Second I wanted is to say THANK YOU for making starting a new business easy. Marsha and Ernie Lankford

Rags to Stitches
Leighton, Alabama

P.S. With the above orders we were able to repay ourselves for all the equipment and supplies we ordered from you. AGAIN THANK YOU!!!

And another one…

Bob,

Thank-you so much for your services. Not only are you helpful, prompt (in returning phone calls) and knowledgeable but also your equipment is great. It really produces quality images and now I have more orders than I can screen! After I bought the book you referred to me I began making t-shirts. Even though I am a full-time college student I still have found time to make a few hundred shirts this year. In the future I will definitely be coming back to upgrade!

Sincerely,
　Ted Kwartler

P.S. Anyone just starting out should get the artwork professionally done. It will save a ton of time and is worth the average of $40 per hour (most of the time it takes less than an hour)!

If you would like a free list of silkscreen materials, suppliers, and/or a free video, please contact us at:

HCB Intl. Enterprises Inc
PO Box 2270
Smithfield, NC 27577
800-311-8962
tshirt@homecashbusiness.com

or visit us at:

www.homecashbusiness.com

Appendix B – Suppliers

Alaska

Image Control Systems
552 W 58th Ave # A
Anchorage, AK 99518
ph: (907) 561-1885   fax: (907) 562-2691

Alabama

Jones Sportswear
1630 2nd Ave South
Birmingham, AL 35233
(800) 762-0719
ph: (205) 326-6264   fax: (205) 324-9647

Screen Process of Alabama LLC
7110 Gadsden Hwy
Trussville, AL 35173
(800) 804-0786
ph: (205) 655-2757   fax: (205) 655-4418

Texsource Inc
911 5th Ave North
Birmingham, AL 35203
(888) 414-7036
ph: (205) 327-8196   fax: (205) 327-8198

Tubelite Company
504 35th North
Birmingham, AL 35222
(800) 331-0321
www.tubelite.com

Arizona

Advanced Screen Technologies
619 S Hacienda Dr # 5
Tempe, AZ 85281
(877) 509-7600
ph: (480) 858-9804   fax: (480) 858-0358

Lukavics & Associates
8586 E Ind School B
Scottsdale, AZ 85252
ph: (602) 502-6976   fax: (602) 947-2053

Multicraft Inc
3233 East Van Buren St
Phoenix, AZ 85008
(800) 442-4244
ph: (602) 244-9444   fax: (602) 275-1135
www.multicraftink.com

Tubelite
4102 W Adams St
Phoenix AZ 85009
(800) 423-0669
ph: (602) 484-0122   fax: (800) 552-2341
www.tubelite.com

California

A-Z Marketing Systems Inc
14639 Titus St
Panorama City, CA 91402
ph: (818) 989-1938   fax: (818) 989-7701

American Eagle Supply Inc
20639 Lycoming St Ste B8
Walnut, CA 91789
ph: (877) 892-3300   fax: (909) 468-5003
www.a-eagle.com

Beckmar Co LLC
1080 N Batavia St Unit E
Orange, CA 92867
(800) 667-1212
ph: (714) 289-4435   fax: (714) 289-4478
www.beckmar.com

Best Screen Supply
1822 S Hill St
Los Angeles, CA 90015
ph: (213) 744-1172   fax: (213) 744-1379

California Sign Supplies
4000 Industrial Way
Benicia, CA 94510
(800) 999-9090
ph: (707) 746-5300   fax: (707) 746-8908

Chem Consultants
1885 S Vineyard Ave Ste # 5
Ontario, CA 91761
ph: (800) 967-4070   fax: (909) 673-1944

Chemical Consultants Inc
1850 Wild Turkey Cir
Corona, CA 92880
ph: (951) 735-5511   fax: (951) 735-7999

CMK Wholesale Products
2361 Prairie St
Chatsworth, CA 91331
ph: (800) 687-4111   fax: (818) 700-9771

Coastal Supply Co Inc
8650 Argent St
Santee, CA 92071
ph: (619) 562-8880   fax: (619) 562-2772

Denco Sales
5447 E Lamona
Fresno, CA 93727
ph: (559) 454-5095   fax: (559) 454-5097

Denco Sales
14042 Central Ave
Chino, CA 91710
ph: (909) 364-8517   fax: (909) 364-8527

Denco Sales Co
1960 Olivera Rd
Concord, CA 94520
(800) 371-7970
ph: (925) 822-0000   fax: (925) 798-5296

Dynamic Screen Supply
1885 S Vineyard Ave # 5
Ontario, CA 91761
(800) 967-4070
ph: (909) 673-1995

J Hopkins Co
17106 E 14th St
Hayward CA 94541
ph: (510) 276-1659   fax: (510) 276-8712
www.hopkinsparts.com

McLogan Supply Co
345 16th St
San Diego, CA 92101-7605
ph: (619) 595-0270   fax: (619) 595-0278

McLogan Supply Co
711 S East St
Anaheim, CA 92805
ph: (714) 999-1194   fax: (714) 999-0195

McLogan Supply Co
2010 South Main St
Los Angeles, CA 90007
(800) 625-6426
ph: (213) 749-2262   fax: (213) 745-6540

Midwest Sign & Screen Printing Supply Co
21054 Alexander Ct
Hayward, CA 94545
(800) 824-2468
ph: (510) 732-5800   fax: (510) 732-7624

Nazdar West
11821 Western Ave
Garden Grove, CA 92841
(800) 258-5050
ph: (714) 894-7578   fax: (714) 891-7875
www.nazdar.com

Parmele Screen Process Supplies
7265 Coldwater Canyon
North Hollywood, CA 91605
ph: (818) 982-9339   fax: (818) 982-2351
www.parmelesupply.com

Resource Group
San Francisco, CA
(866) 845-8228
ph: (510) 552-1682   fax: (209) 845-8467
www.resourcegrp.net

Rheetech Sales and Services Inc
2401 S Main St
Los Angeles, CA 90007
ph: (213) 749-4111   fax: (213) 749-0226
www.prinsupply.com

S&S Screeprinting & Sign Supplies
2231 Sturgis Rd # E
Oxnard, CA 93030
ph: (805) 988-1061   fax: (805) 988-7617

Screen Depot
2123 S Main St
Los Angeles, CA 90007
ph: (213) 747-2727   fax: (213) 746-0092

Screen Printers Resource Inc
2320 E Orangethorpe Ave Ste C
Anaheim, CA 92806
(888) 435-2468
ph: (714) 441-1155   fax: (714) 441-1196
www.spresource.com

Screen Printing Products
22 Beta Ct
San Ramon, CA 94583
(800) 420-9817
ph: (925) 855-9580   fax: (925) 855-9583

Screen Printing Products
4251 Park Rd
Benicia, CA 945110
ph: (707) 745-4465   fax: (707) 745-4460

Screenprinting Products
7939 Silverton Ave Ste 811
San Diego, CA 92126
ph: (858) 547-9997   fax: (858) 547-9998

Sherwood Screen Print Supply
9400 Lyndley Plaza Way
Elk Grove, CA 95624
ph: (916) 714-9696

Tech USA
15 Rockview Dr
Irvine, CA 92612
ph: (949) 679-4996

TW Graphics Group
3323 S Malt Ave
Commerce, CA 90040
(800) 734-1704
ph: (323) 721-1400   fax: (323) 724-2105

Universal Screen Process
8018 E Santa Ana Cyn Rd # 100-161
Anaheim Hills, CA 92808
ph: (310) 293-9268   fax: (714) 993-5561

Westix Equipment & Supply
1309 D Simpson Way
Escondido, CA 92029
ph: (760) 489-1448   fax: (760) 489-7669

Colorado

Denco Sales
55 S Yuma
Denver, CO 80223
(800) 232-0607
ph: (303) 733-0607   fax: (303) 733-2348

Midwest Sign & Screen Printing Supply Co
5301 Peoria St Unit F
Denver, CO 80239
(800) 332-3819
ph: (303) 373-9800   fax: (800) 497-6691

Rocky Mountain Screen Supply
19166 E Carmel Cir
Aurora, CO 80011
(866) 648-6776
ph: (303) 365-2442   fax: (303) 365-2441
www.randysgarage.com

Connecticut

Garston Sign & Screen Printing Supplies
570 Tolland St
East Hartford, CT 6108
(800) 966-9626
ph: (860) 289-3040   fax: (860) 289-3005
www.garston.com

Sharp Products Intl
77 North Plains Industrial Rd
Wallingford, CT 06492
(800) 274-2773
ph: (203) 284-2627   fax: (203)-284-8550
www.sharppro.com

Florida

Florida Flex Ink
2373 W 78th St
Hialeah, FL 33016
ph: (305) 468-0004   fax: (305) 468-0006

Florida Screen Supply
18894 Loblolly Bay Ct
Jupiter, FL 33458
ph: (561) 745-1647   fax: (561) 744-0080

National UV Supply
549 W 13th St
Apopka, FL 32703
(800) 940-6887   fax: (407) 889-0865

Nazdar Miami
16250 NW 59th Ave Ste 205
Miami Lakes, FL 33014
800-788-0554
ph: (305) 817-8280   fax: (305) 817-8284
www.nazdar.com

Press Doctor Enterprises
1928 Tigertail Blvd #12
Dania Beach, FL 33004
ph: (954) 367-3628   fax: (954) 367-3629
www.pressdoctor.net

Rutland
4171 NW 135th St
Opa Locka, FL 33054
(888) 769-9488
ph: (305) 769-9119   fax: (305) 769-9889
www.rutlandinc.com

Screen Process Equipment & Supply
2280 NW 38th Ave
Gainesville, FL 32605
(800) 628-8579
ph: (352) 372-1480   fax: (352) 372-9596

Tubelite - Miami
11205 NW 131st St
Miami, FL 33178
(800) 331-0321
ph: (305) 883-9070   fax: (800) 982-9605
www.tubelite.com

Tubelite - Orlando
102 Semoran Commerce Pl
Apopka, FL 32703
800-505-4900
ph: (407) 884-0477   fax: (800) 445-8823
www.tubelite.com

TW Graphics Group
1175 Florida Central Pkwy # 3000
Longwood, FL 32750
(800) 901-3051
ph: (407) 332-4488   fax: (407) 332-8862

Georgia

Nazdar Atlanta
4260 Peachtree Ind Blvd
Norcross, GA 30071
(800) 537-4606
ph: (770) 476-0510   fax: (770) 623-0297
www.nazdar.com

Reece Supply Co
5755 Oakbrook Pkwy
Norcross , GA 30093
(800) 776-0115   fax: (770) 326-7927
www.reecesupply.com

Xpress Screen Frames
351 Marietta Rd
Canton, GA 30114
(800) 720-1543
ph: (770) 720-1543   fax: (770) 720-9842

Hawaii

American T-Shirt Co
1217 N King St
Honolulu, HI 96817
(800) 494-4073
ph: (808) 842-4466   fax: (808) 842-1911

NSN Hawaii
255 Sand Island Access Rd # 2B
Honolulu, HI 96819
ph: (808) 841-5077

One Shot Supply
815-A Waikamilo Rd
Honolulu HI 96817
ph: (808) 841-7613   fax: (808) 842-0478

Iowa

Screen Printing Supplies Inc
1450 NE 69th Pl Ste 53
Ankeny, IA 50021
(800) 876-7774
ph: (515) 289-3728   fax: (515) 289-3730

Idaho

Denco Sales
605 E 46th St
Boise ID 83714
ph: (208) 375-0100   fax: (208) 375-0103

Illinois

Atlas Screen Supply Co
9353 Seymour Ave
Schiller Park, IL 60176
(800) 621-4173
ph: (847) 233-0515   fax: (847) 233-0506

Dick Blick Co
Rt 150 Knoxville Rd
Galesburg, IL 61401
(800) 447-8192
ph: (309) 343-6181   fax: (309) 343-3399

Nazdar - Midwest
1087 N North Branch St
Chicago, IL 60622
(800) 736-7636
ph: (312) 943-8338   fax: (312) 943-8215
www.nazdar.com

Screenworks Supply Corp
1900 N Austin Ave
Chicago, IL 60639
(800) 551-5524
ph: (773) 836-0940   fax: (773) 836-0950
www.screenworkssupply.com

Indiana

Nazdar - Indianapolis
2910 Fortune Circle W Dr Ste C
Indianapolis, IN 46241
(800) 783-3883
ph: (317) 484-4500   fax: (317) 484-4510
www.nazdar.com

Screenworks Supply Corporation
Richmond, IN 47374
(877) 983-1911
ph: (765) 983-1911   fax: (773) 836-0950

Tubelite - Indianapolis
3875 Culligan Unit H
Indianapolis, IN 46218
(800) 634-5938
ph: (317) 352-9366   fax: (800) 382-1259
www.tubelite.com

Kansas

Nazdar - Kansas
8501 Hedge Lane Terr
Shawnee, KS 66227-3290
(800) 677-4657
ph: (913) 422-1888   fax: (913) 422-2295
www.nazdar.com

SPSI
8302 Hedge Lane Terr Ste H
Shawnee, KS 66227
(800) 876-7774   fax: (913) 422-8304

Kentucky

One Stroke Inks
Louisville, KY
(800) 942-4447

Wolf Printables Inc
Louisville, KY
(800) 882-9653

Louisiana

Reece Supply Co
1012 Distributors Row
Harahan, LA 70123
(800) 776-0130
ph: (504) 733-7799   fax: (504) 736-0056

Masaschusettes

Etchomatic Inc
179 Olde Canal Dr
Lowell, MA 01851-2732
(800) 634-3006
ph: (978) 656-0011   fax: (978) 656-9903

Garston Sign & Screen Printing Inc
21 Parkridge Rd
Haverhill, MA 01835
(800) 328-7775
ph: (978) 374-0600   fax: (978) 374-9777
www.garston.com

Lambert Co
1400 Providence Hwy Ste 3000
Norwood, MA 2062
(800) 292-2900
ph: (781) 440-0842   fax: (781) 440-0874

Maryland

Martin Supply Co Inc
2740 Loch Raven Rd
Baltimore, MD 21218
(800) 282-5440   fax: (410) 366-0134

Michigan

Advanced Screen Products Plus
1400 Front St NW Ste C
Grand Rapids, MI 49504
(877) 379-3700
ph: (616) 774-3348   fax: (616) 774-3435

Desmond Process Supply Co Inc
2277 Elliott Ave
Troy, MI 48083
(800) 968-1115
ph: (248) 589-9100   fax: (248) 589-0038
www.desmondpro.com

Nazdar Michigan
687 Minnesota Ave
Troy, MI 48083
ph: (248) 588-4900   fax: (248) 588-0370
www.nazdar.com

One Stop
2686 Northridge Dr NW
Grand Rapids, MI 49544
(800) 968-7550
ph: (616) 784-0404   fax: (616) 784-6264

Screen Grafex Supply
324 Market Ave SW
Grand Rapids, MI 49503
(800) 237-5380
ph: (616) 456-9862   fax: (616) 456-5314

Minnesota

Advantage Supply
850 East Main St
Anoka, MN 55303
(866) 421-7194
ph: (763) 421-7194   fax: (763) 421-7698

Northwest Graphic Supply
4200 E Lake St
Minneapolis, MN 55406
(800) 221-4079
ph: (612) 729-7361   fax: (612) 729-6647

Screen Printing Supplies Inc
9825 85th Ave N Ste 100
Maple Grove, MN 55369
(800) 876-7774
ph: (763) 391-7390   fax: (763) 391-7392
www.sps-i.biz

Missouri

Gateway Screen Products
1806 W Osage St
Pacific, MO 63069
(877) 271-8391   fax: (636) 257-6281

Lawson Screen & Digital Products Inc
5110 Penrose St
Saint Louis, MO 63115
(800) 325-8317
ph: 314-382-9300   fax: (314) 382-3012
www.lawsonsp.com

Midest Sign & Screen Printing
4949 E 59th St
Kansas City, MO 64130
(800) 233-3770
ph: (816) 333-5224   fax: (816) 333-5446

Ryan Screen Supply
712 Fannie Ave
Saint Louis, MO 63125
(800) 769-9130
ph: (314) 631-8753   fax: (314) 631-0635
www.ryanrss.com

North Carolina

Innovative Print Technologies
227 Olympic St
Charlotte, NC 28273
ph: (704) 504-1072

Nazdar - North Carolina
7001-C Cessna Dr
Greensboro, NC 27409-9329
(800) 426-0290
ph: (336) 668-4085   fax: (336) 668-4174
www.nazdar.com

TexSource Inc
301 S Battleground Ave
King Mountain, NC 28086
(888) 344-4657
ph: (704) 739-9612   fax: (704) 739-9688
www.texsourceonline.com

Tubelite - North Carolina
10700 Twin Lakes Parkway
Charlotte, NC 28269
(800) 438-1044
ph:(704) 875-3117   fax: (800) 321-4881
www.tubelite.com

XpressScreen
930 Burke St
Winston-Salem, NC 27101
(800) 597-9530
ph: (336) 722-2500   fax: (336)-722-2575

Nebraska

Midwest Sign and Screen Printing
9313 J St
Omaha, NE 68127
(800) 228-3839
ph: (402) 592-7555   fax: (800) 228-3886

New Jersey

Charles M Jessup Inc
177 Smith St
Keasbey, NJ 08832-0159
(800) 525-4657
ph: (732) 324-0430   fax: (732) 324-1616

Nazdar - New Jersey
7055 Central Hwy
Pennsauken, NJ 8109
(800) 257-8226
ph: (856) 663-7878   fax: (856) 663-9467
www.nazdar.com

Performance Screen Supply LLC
919 Route 33
Freehold, NJ 7728
(800) 659-8337
ph: (732) 866-6081   fax: (800) 808-8337
www.performancescreen.com

Tubelite - New Jersey
300 E Park St
Moonachie, NJ 7074
(800) 631-0778
ph: (201) 641-1011   fax: (800) 637-1011
www.tubelite.com

Union Ink Co Inc
453 Broad Ave
Ridgefield, NJ 7657
(800) 526-0455
ph: (201) 945-5766   fax: (201) 945-4111

New Mexico

Denco Sales
3430 Princeton Dr NE
Albuquerque, NM 87107
ph: (505) 830-0212   fax: (505) 830-0213

Nevada

Screen Print Resource Inc
6575 Hinson
Las Vegas, NV 89118
ph: (714) 441-1155   fax: (714) 441-1196

Triangle Ink Co
5360 Procyon St
Las Vegas, NV 89118-2444
(800) 224-0464
ph: (702) 597-5990   fax: (702) 597-5993

New York

Buffalo Printers Supply Inc
3 Peuquet Pkwy
Buffalo, NY 14150
(800) 344-4024
ph: (716) 693-7000   fax: (716) 693-7774

Commercial Art Supply
3333 W Henrietta Rd
Henrietta, NY 14623
ph: (716) 427-9290   fax: (716) 427-9146

Commercial Art Supply
935 Erie Blvd E
Syracuse, NY 13210
(800) 669-2787
ph: (315) 474-1000   fax: (315) 474-531

Davis International
388 Mason Rd Ste 1A
Fairport, NY 14450
ph: (585) 421-8175   fax: (585) 421-8707

Garston Sign & Screen Printing Inc
180 Commerce Dr
Rochester, NY 14623
(800) 825-8808
ph: (585) 321-1610   fax: (585) 321-1665
www.garston.com

Pearl Art & Craft
308 Canal St
New York, NY 10013
(800) 221-6845
ph: (212) 431-7932   fax: (212) 431-6798

R Jennings Mfg Co Inc
22 Hudson Falls Rd
South Glens Falls, NY 12803
(800) 500-2279   fax: (518) 798-3172

Reich Supply Co
2 Campion Rd
New Hartford, NY 13413
(800) 338-3322
ph: (315) 732-6126   fax: (315) 732-7841
www.reichsupply.com

Saati Print
247 Route 100
Somers, NY 10589
(800) 431-2200
ph: (914) 232-7781   fax: (914) 232-4004

Standard Screen Supply Corp
121 Varick St
New York, NY 10013
(800) 221-2697
ph: (212) 627-2727   fax: (212) 627-2770
www.standardscreen.com

Victory Factory
184-10 Jamaica Ave
Hollis, NY 11423
(800)255-5335
ph: (718) 454-2255   fax: (718)454-2255

Ohio

Multicraft Inc
4701 Lakeside Ave
Cleveland, OH 44114
(800) 742-8000
ph: (216) 432-5656   fax: (216) 432-5757
www.multicraftink.com

Nazdar - Ohio
3905 Port Union Rd
Fairfield, OH 45014
(800) 729-9942
ph: (513) 870-5706   fax: (513) 870-5713
www.nazdar.com

Off Contact Productions
1501 Monroe St
Toledo, OH 43624
ph: (419) 255-5546   fax: (419) 255-4440

Printer's Edge
4965 Mahoning Ave
Warren, OH 44483
(800) 467-3343
ph: (330) 372-2232   fax: (330) 372-3727

Richardson Supply Inc
2080 Hardy Parkway
Grove City, OH 43123
(800) 635-7695
ph: (614) 539-3033   fax: (614) 539-3032

Rutland
777-B Dearborn Park Ln
Worthington, OH 43085
(866) 788-5263
ph: (614) 846-3055   fax: (614) 846-3943
www.rutlandinc.com

Tubelite
1224 Refugee Ln
Columbus, OH 43207
(800) 848-0576
ph: (614) 443-9734   fax: 800-822-299
www.tubelite.com

Okalahoma

Graphic Solutions Group
6731 S Eastern Ave
Oklahoma City OK 73149
(800) 677-3149   fax: (800) 747-1430

Graphic Supply Co
1131 S 71st Ave E
Tulsa, OK 74112-5601
(800) 234-0765
ph: (918) 836-6524   fax: (918) 836-4854
www.graphicsupplyinc.com

Industrial Screen & Sign Supply LLC
5432 S 103 E Ave
Tulsa, OK 74146
(866) 664-2226
ph: (918) 664-2226   fax: (866) 664-2226

Reece Supply Co - Tulsa
3148 S 108th East Ave Ste 130
Tulsa, OK 74146
(800) 520-2300
ph: (918) 556-5000   fax: (918) 556-5001

South Western Process Supply Co
1414 E 3rd St
Tulsa, OK 74120
(800) 858-8211
ph: (918) 582-8211   fax: (918) 582-0066

Southwestern Process Supply Co
304 N Meridian Ste 9
Oklahoma City, OK 73107
(800) 858-8211
ph: (405) 942-8658   fax: (405) 942-8499

Oregon

Denco Sales Co
2119 SE 11th Ave
Portland, OR 97214
(800) 345-0172
ph: (503) 235-0460   fax: (503) 235-0468

Midwest Sign & Screen Printing Supply Co
5035 NW Front St
Portland, OR 97210
(800) 228-0596
ph: (503) 224-1400   fax: (503) 224-6400

Northwest Sign Supply
602 SE Salmon
Portland, OR 97214
(800) 873-0111
ph: (503) 233-0111   fax: (503) 235-4437

Wahkeena Northwest Sales
PO Box 90785
Portland, OR 97290
(800) 760-0802   fax: (503) 760-0891
www.Wahkeena.com

Pennsylvania

Enovation Graphic Systems Inc
2403 Sideny St
Pittsburgh, PA 15203
(800) 463-2731
ph: (412) 922-1333   fax: (412) 922-0510

Pocono Mt Screen Supply Inc
Two Chapel St
Honesdale, PA 18431
(888) 637-4835
ph: (570) 253-6375   fax: (570) 253-1978
www.poconoscreen.com

Wild Side North Inc
107 Arrowhead Dr
Slippery Rock, PA 16057
(888) 245-3810
ph: (724) 794-4100   fax: (724) 794-1243
www.wildsidenorth.com

Tennessee

Tubelite - Tennessee
3111 Bellbrook Dr
Memphis, TN 38116
(800) 238-5280
ph: (901) 396-8320   fax: (901) 396-4648
www.tubelite.com

Texas

Graphic Solutions Group
304 N Walton St
Dallas, TX 75226
(800) 366-1776   fax: (800) 676-0034
www.gsginet.com

Graphic Solutions Group
1293 N Post Oak Ste 190
Houston TX 77055
(800) 775-7545   fax: (713) 957-0310
www.gsginet.com

Herweck's
300 Broadway
San Antonio, TX 78205
(800) 725-1349
ph: (210-227-1349   fax: (210-227-8533
www.herwecks.com

Lee's Screen Process Supply Co
10440 W Airport Blvd
Stafford, TX 77477
(800) 447-8874
ph: (281) 879-5337   fax: (281) 568-8756

McBee Supply
6100 Skyline Ste J
Houston, TX 77057
(800) 622-3304
ph: (713) 972-1388   fax: 713-972-1385
www.mcbeesupply.com

Reece Supply Co
4955 Stout Dr
San Antonio, TX 78219
(800) 776-0224
ph: (210) 662-6898   fax: (210) 662-6945

Reece Supply Co
2606 Bell
Houston, TX 77003
(800) 776-0113
ph: (713) 228-9496   fax: (713) 228-9499

Reece Supply Co
3308 Royalty Row
Irving, TX 75062
(800) 776-7448
ph: (972) 438-3131   fax: (972) 721-1758

Reece Supply Co
1530 Goodyear Ste J
El Paso, TX 79936
(877) 776-0128
ph: (915) 592-9600   fax: (915) 592-9050

Utah

Intermountain Embroidery
10338 South 460 East
Sandy, UT 84670
(888) 437-8473   fax: (801) 571-8274

Midwest Sign & Screen Printing Supply Co
1160 S Pioneer Rd Ste 2
Salt Lake City, UT 84104
(800) 497-6690
ph: (801) 974-9449   fax: (800) 497-6691

Performance Screen Supply LLC
530 West 9460 South Ste D
Sandy, UT 84070
(800) 659-8337
ph: (801) 569-1001   fax: (800) 808-8337
www.performancescreen.com

Regional Sign Supply
3571 S 300 West
Salt Lake City, UT 84115

(800) 365-8920
ph: (801) 262-6451   fax: (801) 261-5658
www.regionalsupply.net

Technical Service & Supply
2465 SW Temple
Salt Lake City, UT 84115
(800) 895-7697
ph: (801) 467-7832   fax: (801) 467-7889

Virginia

CMO Sign Surfaces
2941 Walmsley Blvd
Richmond VA 23234
(800) 888-4844
ph: (804) 743-1488   fax: (804) 271-4664

The Art Market
1517 W Broad St
Richmond, VA 23220
(800) 541-3697
ph: (804) 353-7893   fax: (804) 359-2774

Washington

Denco Sales
711 S Fidalgo
Seattle, WA 98108
ph: (206) 764-9180   fax: (206) 764-9214

Dimensional Products Corporation
1467 Elliott Ave West
Seattle, WA 98119
(800) 782-3801
ph: (206) 352-9065   fax: (206) 352-8042
www.dimensionalproducts.com

JSMD Key Products
6323 83rd Ave SE
Snohomish, WA 98290
ph: (360) 568-8469

Midwest Sign & Screen Printing Supply Co
401 Evans Black Dr
Seattle, WA 98118
(800) 426-4938
ph: (206) 433-8080   fax: (206) 433-8021

Northwest Sign Supply Inc East
15916 Sprague Ave
Veradale, WA 99037
(800) 678-7923
ph: (509) 927-7943   fax: (509) 927-8196

Northwest Sign Supply Inc
5300 4th Ave S
Seattle, WA 98108
(800) 654-0194
ph: (206) 767-9592   fax: (206) 767-9675

Ryonet Corp
11410 NE 72nd Ave
Vancouver, WA 98686
(800) 314-6390
fax: (360) 546-1454 www.silkscreeningsupplies.com

Silk Screen Frames
11653 Higgins Airport Wa
Burlington, WA 98233
(800) 574-3477
ph: (360) 757-2102   fax: (360) 757-4417
www.silkscreenframes.com

Wisconsin

Badger Graphic Sales
1225 Delanglade St
Kaukauna, WI 54130
(800) 558-5350
ph: (920) 766-9332   fax: (920) 766-3081

Midwest Sign & Screen Printing Supply Co
10061 South 54th St
Franklin, WI 53132-9185
(800) 242-7430
ph: (414) 423-1200   fax: (800) 242-7439

Northland Graphics Inc
N 11016 County A
Tomahawk, WI 54487
(800) 826-0100
ph: (715) 453-5166   fax: (715) 453-5507

Screen Printing Supplies Inc
N 19 W6725 Commerce Ct
Cedarburg, WI 53012
(800) 876-7774
ph: (262) 387-9930   fax: (262) 387-9940

SSPS Spectrum Inc
W228 S6938 Enterprise Dr
Big Ben, WI 53103
ph: (262) 662-1700   fax: (262) 662-3850

Valley Litho Supply Co
1047 Haugen Ave
Rice Lake, WI 54868
(800) 826-6781
ph: (715) 234-1525   fax: (715) 234-6813

Garments

Alore
2503 Neergard
Springfield, MO 65803
(800) 375-4011   fax: (417) 865-5202
www.alore.net

Alpha Shirt Company
www.alphashirt.com

American Apparel
USA
    747 Warehouse St
    Los Angeles, CA 90021
ph: (213) 488-0226   fax: (213) 488-0334

Canada
    350 Louvain #203
    Montreal, QUE H2N-2E8
ph: (514) 939-0245   fax: (514) 939-0695
www.americanapparel.net

Americana Online Store
CA
    18150 S Figeroa St
    Gardina CA, 90248
    (800) 473-2802
ph: (310) 354-1380   fax: (310) 354-1386
Corporate: (310) 354-1377
CO
    5901 E 58th Ave
    Commerce City, CO 80022
    (800) 822-5520
ph: (303) 287-7481   fax: (303) 287-0640
OK
    3120 N Sante Fe
    Oklahoma City, OK 73118
    (800) 397-5396
ph: (405) 557-0004   fax: (405) 525-8115
www.americanasportswear.com

Atlantic Coast Cotton Printable Sportswear
(800) 262-5660
www.atlanticcoastcotton.com

Atlanta Tees Inc
(800) 554-1079
www.atlantatees.com

Banzai Creations
417 Boot Rd
Downingtown, PA 19335
(800) 786-0162
ph: (610) 873-9710   fax: (610) 873-6882
www.webdyes.com

Beneficial T's
(800) 676-5546
fax: (775) 746-7808
www.beneficialts.com

Blue Mountain Sportswear
811 Alpha Dr Ste #339
Richard, TX 75081
(972) 907-0209
ph: (972) 907-0389   fax: (972) 907-0187
E-Fax(425) 977-7104
www.bluemountainsportswear.com

Bodek and Rhodes
(800) 523-2721
fax: (800) 531-9626
www.bodekandrhodes.com

Broder Bros.
www.broderbros.com

Continental Sportswear
135 West 27th St
New York, NY 10001
(800) 543-5007   fax: (212) 966-5720

www.continentalsportswear.com

Dharma Trading Co
(800) 542-5227
www.dharmatrading.com

Dye Masters
1765 E Jacinto Cir
Mesa, AZ 85204
(877) NICE-DYE   (6423-393)
www.dyemasters.net

Eva Tees
Eva Tees Inc
48-40 34th St
Long Island City, NY 11101-2516
(800) EVA-TEES (382-8337)
fax: (888) FAX-TEES (329-8337)
Administrative Offices:
ph: (718) 729-1260   fax: (718) 729-1824
www.evatees.com

Georgia Tees
Apparel & Accessories
PO Drawer T
4200 McEver Industrial Blvd
Acworth, GA 30101
(800) 553-0021
ph: (770) 974-0040   fax: (770) 975-9705
(800) 782-6268
www.gatees.com

Gilden Active Wear
Gildan Corprate Head Quarters
725 Montée de Liesse
Montréal, Québec, Canada H4T1P5
(800) 668-8337
fax: (514) 735-2024
www.gildan.com

Gildan Activewear SRL
Gildan House
34 Warrens
St Michael, Barbados
(877) 445-3265
ph: (246) 421-7751   fax: (246) 421-7780

Golden State T's
Golden State T's
1404 South 7th St
San Jose, CA 95112
(800) 892-8337
ph: (408) 278-1212   fax: (408) 278-1220
www.goldenstatetees.com

Hanes
Mailing
    PO Box 15901
    Winston-Salem, NC 27103
Shipping
    1000 E Hanes Mill Rd
    Winston-Salem, NC 27105
(800) 685-7557
fax: (800) 289-1870
www.hanesprintables.com

Imprint Wholesale
CO
    6795 Sandown Rd
    Denver, CO 80216
    (800) 634-2945
ph: (303) 333-3200   fax: (303) 333-7373
WA
    5822 South 196th St
    Kent, WA 98032
    (800) 659-9465
ph: (253) 437-1158   fax: (253) 437-2031
NV
    3290 W Sunset Rd #C
    Las Vegas, NV 89118
    (800) 964-9031

ph: (702) 896-4666   fax: (702) 896-4867
www.imprintswholesale.com

Jerzees
Corporate Offices: JERZEES
Division of Russell Corporation
3350 Cumberland Blvd Ste 1000
Atlanta, GA 30339
ph: (678) 742-8000
www.jerzees.com

Kaymen
Anaheim, CA
1680 Gene Autry Way
Anaheim, CA 92805
ph: (714) 978-6655   fax: (714) 978-6633
S San Francisco
1335 Lowrie Ave
S San Francisco, CA 94080
ph: (650) 589-8900   fax: (650) 589-5686
CO
4901 Ironton St
Denver, CO 80239
ph: (303) 375-1400   fax: (303) 375-0075
AZ
836 E University Dr
Phoenix, AZ 85034
ph: (602) 269-1300   fax: (602) 256-7555
www.kayman.com

LA Loving
415 Eleventh Ave South
Hopkins, MN 55343-7843
            (800) 328-5927
ph: (952) 912-2500   fax: (952) 912-2525
fax: (800) 370-8706
www.laloving.com

McCreary's Tees
Customer Service
McCreary's Tees

4121 East Raymond St
Phoenix, AZ 85040
www.mccrearystees.com

Mission Imprintables
Customer Service
Mission Imprintables Inc
7130 Miramar Rd Ste 400
San Diego, CA 92121
(800) 480-0800
www.missionimprintables.com

Morija
Unit 6, Brandon Industrial Estate
Brandon Rd, London N7 9AA
ph: 00-44 (0) 207-609-398
www.morija.com

Nogar.com
HANCO M Handelsman Company
1323 S Michigan Ave
Chicago IL 60605
(800) 938-6917
www.nogar.com

One Stop Imprintable Fashions
www.onestopinc.com

Paw Distribution
www.pawdist.com
PAW Distributors
27 Dwight Pl
Fairfield, NJ 07004
(800) 524-0664
ph: (973) 575-2511   fax: (973) 575-1928

Perfect Junior Basics
Northern California
Richard Dash   (831) 426-1824
Southern California
Kevin Quinn   (213) 626-2026

(213) 910-8192
www.surfnetusa.com

Print Gear Sports Wear Distribution
1769 Airport Blvd
Cayce, SC 29033
(800) 763-7763
ph: (803) 791-7763   fax: (803) 791-1956
www.printgear.com

Running Wild
Running Strong Inc
DBA Running Wild
506 E Juanita Ave Ste #1
Mesa, AZ 85204

SAC Distributers
Southern Apparel Corporation
12420 73rd Ct North
Largo, FL 33773
(800) 937-TEES
www.sactees.com

Stardust
(800) 747-4444
www.estardust.com

Staton Corporate and Casual
ph: (800) 888-8888   fax: (800) 456-5959
Dallas
ph: (972) 448-3000   fax: (972) 448-3003
Dallas Warehouse   (972) 448-3094
      14275 Welch Rd
      Dallas, TX 75244
Chicago Warehouse   (708) 681-9920
      1600 N 25th Ave Ste C
      Melrose Park, IL 60161
Fullerton Warehouse (714) 680-5422
      701B Burning Tree Rd
      Fullerton, CA 92833
Memphis Warehouse (901) 362-5554

4319 Delp St
Memphis, TN 38118
Orlando Warehouse   (407) 855-8301
    1264 La Quinta Dr
    Orlando FL 32809
www.statonwholesale.com

T-Shirts.com
(800) 588-1857
ph: (847) 932-3900   Fax: (847) 327-9369
www.t-shirts.com

TSM T-shirts and More
7667 National Turnpike Building A
Louisville, KY 40214
(800) 944-4480
ph: (502) 992-1934   fax: (800) 992-0135
www.tshirtsandmore.com

Trade Shows

Awards Expo
A&E Magazine
PO Box 1416
Broomfield, CO 80038
ph: (303) 469-0424   fax: (303) 469-5730
www.nbm.com

Bobbin Group
Bobbin Group of Bill Communications
PO Box 612768
Dallas, TX 75261-2768
Information about exhibiting
(800) 693-1363
ph: (972) 906-6640   fax: (972) 906-6642

Information about attending
(800) 789-2223
ph: (972) 906-6800   fax: (972) 906-6890
Publications
        Bobbin Magazine / La Bobina Magazine
        PO Box 1986
        Columbia, SC 29202
(800) 845-8820
ph: (803) 771-7500   fax: (803) 799-1461
www.bobbin.com

Embroidery Expo
PO Box 40079
Phoenix, AZ 85067
ph: (480) 990-1101   fax: (480) 990-6890
www.vpico.com

The Imprinted Sportswear Show
1199 S Belt Line Rd #100
Coppel, TX 75091
(800) 527-0207
ph: (214) 239-3060   fax: (214) 419-7825
www.issshows.com

Miller-Freeman International Trade Shows
1199 S Belt Line Rd #100
Coppel, TX 75091
(800) 527-0207
ph: (972) 906-6500   fax: (927) 906-6511
www.mfi.com

NBM Inc. Trade Show Producers
www.nbm.com

Print Wear
NBM Shows, Dept 814
Denver, CO 80291
(800) 669-0424
ph: (303) 469-0424   fax: (303) 469-5730
www.nbm.com

SGIA
Screenprinting & Graphic Imaging
Association International
10015 Main St
Fairfax, VA 22031-3489
(888) 385-3588
ph: (703) 385-1335   fax: (703) 273-0456
www.sgia.org

Sports Expo
National Sporting Goods Association International
1699 Wall St
Mt Prospect, IL 60056
(800) 288-1600

Super Show
Sporting Goods Manufacturing Association
1450 NE 123rd St
N Miami, FL 33161
(407) 842-4100

Trade Associations

Advertising Specialty Institute
1120 Wheeler Way
Langhorne, PA 19047
(800) 326-7378
fax: (800) 829-9240
www.promomart.com

Embroidery Trade Association
PO Box 612288
Dallas, TX 75261-2288
(800) 727-3014
ph: (972) 906-6720   fax: (972) 906-6722

www.embroiderytrade.org

Graphic Artists Guild
11 West 20th St 8th Fl
New York, NY 10011-3704
ph: (212) 463-7730

Graphics Arts Technical Foundation
200 Deer Run Rd
Sewickley, PA 15143
ph: (412) 741-6860

National Sporting Goods Association
1699 Wall St
Mt Prospect, IL 60056
(800) 288-1600

Personal & Identification Association
5342 Reese Ave
Fresno, CA 93722
(800) 276-8428
ph: (559) 276-8494   fax: (559) 276-8496
www.personalizedproducts.org

PPAI Promotional Products Association International
PO Box 40079
Phoenix, AZ 85067
(888) 492-6891
www.ppa.org

REI Recognition & Engraving Institute
4323 N Golden State Blvd #105
Fresno, CA 93722
(800) 832-9676
fax: (209) 275-8023

Rochester Institute of Technology
College of Imaging Service
67 Lomb Memorial Dr
Rochester, NY 14623-5603
(800) 724-2536 ext. #32

ph: (716) 475-5000   fax: (716) 475-7000
www.rit.edu/cims/te

SGIA
Screenprinting & Graphic Imaging
Association International
10015 Main St
Fairfax, VA 22031-3489
(888) 385-3588
ph: (703) 385-1335   fax: (703) 273-0456
www.sgia.org

Society of Glass & Ceramic Decorators
1627 K St #800
Washington, DC 200006
ph: (202) 728-4132   fax: (202) 728-4133
www.sgcd.org

SPA Screen Printing Website
Screen Printing Association (UK) Limited
Association House
7a West St
Reigate, Surrey RH2 9BL
(09061) 572572
www.martex.co.uk/screen-printing/

Speacialty Advertising Association International
3125 Skyway Cir N
Irving, TX 75038
ph: (214) 252-0404

Technical Association of the Graphic Arts
68 Lomb Memorial Dr
Rochester, NY 14623
ph: (716) 475-7470   fax: (716) 475-2250

Trade Magazines

Airbrush Action
PO Box
Lakewood, NJ 08701
(800) 232-8998
ph: (732) 364-2111   fax: (732) 367-5908
www.airbrushaction.com

Awards & Engraving
PO Box 1416
Broomfield, CO 80038
ph: (303) 469-0424   fax: (303) 469-5730
www.nbm.com

Corporate Logo
Virgo Publishing, Inc
PO Box 40079
Phoenix, AZ 85067-0079
ph: (480) 990-1101   fax: (480) 990-0819
www.corporatelogo.com

Embroidery Business News
Virgo Publishing, Inc
PO Box 40079
Phoenix, AZ 85067
ph: (480) 990-1101   fax: (480) 990-0819
www.ebnmag.com

Embroidery/Monogram Business
1199 S Beltline Rd Ste 100
Coppell, TX 75019
(800) 527-0207
fax: (847) 647-5972
www.embmag.com

The Engravers Journal
26 Summit St
PO Box 1230
Brighton, MI 48116

ph: (313) 227-2614
(313) 229-8320

Flash Magazine
Riddle Pond Rd
West Topsham, VT 05086
(800) 252-2599
ph: (802) 439-6462   fax: (802) 439-6463
www.flashweb.com

Hat Business Quarterly
Virgo Publishing Inc
PO Box 40079
Phoenix, AZ 85067-0079
ph: (480) 990-1101   fax: (480) 990-0819
www.hbq.com

Impressions Magazine
1199 S Beltline Rd Ste 100
Coppell, TX 75019
(800) 527-0207
fax: (847) 647-5972
www.impressionsmag.com

P and I News
5342 N Reese
Fresno, CA 93722
(209) 276-8494
(209) 276-8496

The Press Magazine
5680 Greenwood Plaza Blvd #100
Englewood, CO 80111
ph: (720) 741-2901   fax: (720) 489-3225
www.thepress.com

Printwear Magazine
2800 Midway
Broomfield, CO 80020
(800) 669-0424
ph: (303) 469-0424   fax: (303) 469-5730

www.nbm.com

Publish (Desktop Publishing/Graphics)
PO Box 2002
Skokie, IL 60076
(847) 588-2540
www.publish.com

Recognition Review
Awards and Recognition Association
4700 W Lake Ave
Glenview, IL 60025-1485
(800) 344-2148
fax: (847) 375-6309
www.amctec.com

The Retailor
4323 N Golden State Blvd #105
Fresno, CA 93722
(800) 832-9676
ph: (209) 275-8023

Screen Graphics Magazine
PO Box 1416
Broomfield, CO 80038
ph: (303) 469-0424   fax: (303) 469-5730
www.nbm.com

Screenprinting Magazine
407 Gilbert Ave
Cincinnati, OH 45202
ph: (513) 421-2050   fax: (513) 421-5144
www.stpubs.com

SGIA Tabloid and Journal
1005 Main St
Fairfax, VA 22031
ph: (703) 385-1335
(703) 273-0456

Sporting Goods Business
PO Box 1782
Riverton, NJ 08077

Stitches Magazine
5680 Greenwood Plaza Blvd #100
Englewood, CO 80111
ph: (720) 489-3190
(720) 489-3225
www.stitches.com

Wearables
5680 Greenwood Plaza #100
Englewood, CO 80111
(303) 741-2901
(720) 489-3225

Emulsion Manufacturers

Autotype Americas Inc
2050 Hammond Dr
Schaumburg, IL 60173-3810
(800) 323-0632
ph: (847) 303-5900   fax: (847) 303-6803
www.autotype.com

Chromaline Corp
4832 Grand Ave
Duluth, MN 55807
(800) 328-4261
ph: (218) 628-2217   fax: (248) 628-3245
www.chromaline.com

Kiwo Inc
1929 Marvin Cir

Seabrook, TX 77586
(800) KIWO-USA
ph: (281) 474-9777   fax: (281) 474-7325
www.kiwo.com

Murakami Screen USA Inc
745 Monterey Pass Rd
Monterey Park, CA 91754
(800) 562-3534
ph: (323) 980-0662   fax: (323) 980-0659
www.murakamiscreen.com

Saati Group
PO Box 440 Rt 100
Somers, NY 10589
(800) 431-2200
ph: (914) 232-7781   fax: (914) 232-4004
www.Saati.com

Ulano Corporation
www.ulano.com

Ink Manufacturers

Amanda System
In House Produced Films
www.amandainks.com

Coates Screen Inc
2445 Production Dr
Saint Charles, IL 60174
(800) 333-4657
ph: (630) 513-5348   fax: (630) 513-1655
www.coates.com

Color Change
1740 Cortland Ct #A
Addison, IL 60101
ph: (630) 705-1000   fax: (630) 705-1010
www.colorchange.com

Excaliber Technologically Superior Ink
Canada
311 Saulteaux Crescent
Winnipeg, MB, Canada R3J 3C7
ph: (204) 885-7792   fax: (204) 831-0426
1-145 Riviera Dr
Markham, ON, L3R5J6 Canada
ph: (905) 470-0744   fax: (905) 470-9454
www.lancergroup.com

International
Box 329, 231-3rd St
Pembina, ND 58271
(800) 665-4875
fax: (204) 831-0426
Asia
Rm L, 5/F, Camelpaint Building,
60 Hoi Yuen Rd
Kwun Tong, Kowloon, Hong Kong
ph: (852) 2790 8313   fax: (852) 2 341 1235

International Coatings
13929 E 166th St
Cerritos, CA 90702-7666
(800) 423-4103
ph: (562) 926-1010   fax: (562) 926-9486
Dalton, GA
ph: (706) 277-7794   fax: (706) 277-7803
www.iccink.com

Multi-Tech Inc
5101 Penrose St
St Louis, MO 63115
ph: (314) 382-9881   fax: (314) 382-5637

Nazdar Co
8501 Hedge Lane Terr
Shawnee, KS 66227
(800) 767-942
ph: (913) 422-1888   fax: (913) 422-2295
Chicago, IL   (800) 736-7636
Garden Grove, CA   (800) 252-7767
Medley, FL   (800) 788-0554
Pennsauken, NJ   (800) 257-8226
www.nazdar.com

Pavonine Products
316 N Main St
Lynchburg, OH 45142
(800) 817-8732
www.pavonine.com

Polyone
US/Canada   (800) 735-4353
International   (770) 590-3500
www.wilflex.com

Rutland Plastics
PO Box 339
10021 Rodney Street
Pineville, NC 28134
(800) 438-5134
ph: (704) 553-0046   fax: (704) 552-6589
www.rutlandinc.com

Triangle Ink
53-57 Van Dyke St
Wallington, New Jersey 07057
(800) 524-1592
ph: (201) 935-2777   fax: (201) 935-5961
www.triangleink.com

Union Ink
(800) 526-0455
ph: (201) 945-5766   fax: (201) 945-4111
www.unionink.com

TW Graphics Group
West Coast   saleswc@twgraphics.com
32323 S Malt Ave
Commerce, CA 90040
(800) 247-5589
ph: (323) 721-1400   fax: (323) 724-2105
East Coast: salesec@twgraphics.com
1175 Florida Central Pkwy #3000
Longwood, FL 32750
(800) 262-3051
ph: (407) 332-4488   fax: (407) 332-8862
www.twgraphics.com

Heat Transfers

Ace Customer Transfer Co
334 North Mulberry St
PO Box 202
Tremont City, OH 45372
ph: (800) 525-3126   fax: (800) 434-0468
ph: (937) 969-8335   fax: (937) 969-8136
www.acetransco.com

Alpha Supply
Mailing
PO Box 60600
Nashville, TN 37206
Shipping
3510 Golf St #4
Nashville, TN 37216
(800) 908-9916
www.alphasupply.com

BRN Corporation

Route 3
RR1 Box 827
Thornton, NH 03223
ph: (603) 726-3800   fax: (603) 726-3870
www.brncorp.com

Conde
Conde Systems, Inc
7851 Schillinger Park West
Mobile, AL 36608-9697
(800) 826-6332
ph: (251) 633-5704   fax: (251) 633-3876
www.conde.com

Geo Knight & Co Inc
54 Lincoln St
Brockton MA 02301
(800) 525-6766
ph: (508) 588-0186   fax: (508) 587-5108
www.geoknight.com

HIX Corp
1201 E 27th St
Pittsburgh, KS 66762
(800) 835-0606
ph: (316) 231-8568   fax: (316) 231-1598
www.hixcorp.com

Impulse Wear
225 Business Center Dr
Blacklick, OH 43004
(800) 255-1280
www.impulsewear.com

Jesse J Heap & Son
576 South 21st St
Irvington, NJ 07111-4202
ph: (973) 372-1559   fax: (973) 372-1929
www.jesseheap.com

Juto Parapoy Image Trans
Joto Paper Inc - USA
    1125 Fir Ave
    Blaine, WA, 98230
Joto Paper Ltd - Canada
    1625 Ingleton Ave
    Burnaby, BC V5C 4L8
(800) 565-5686
ph: (604) 320-1803   fax: (800) 565-5622
www.jotopaper.com

Pro Distributers
5135 A 69th St
Lubbock, TX 79424
(800) 658-2027
ph: (806) 794-3692   fax: (806) 794-9699
www.prodistributors.com

Pro World
Pro World
1000 Taylors Ln
Cinnaminson, NJ 08077
(800) 678-8289
fax: (888) 303-6345
International   (856) 303-2777
International Fax   (856) 303-2778
www.proworldinc.com

Sawgrass Systems
Sawgrass Systems, Inc
c/o Sales & Marketing
2233 Highway 17 N
Mt Pleasant, SC 29466-6806
ph: (843) 884-1575   fax: (843) 849-3847
www.sublimation.com

Stahls Inc
(800) 521-9702
fax: (800) 346-2216
www.stahls.com

Sun Art Design Inc
USA Main Office
2800 N 29 Ave
Hollywood, FL 33020
(800) 771-7786
ph: (954) 929-6622   fax: (954) 929-5447
European Sales Office
ph: (972) 3973-3770   fax: (972) 3973-3303

Transfer Technology
Transfer Technology
Division BRN Corporation
RR1 Box 827 US Route 3
Thornton, NH 03223
(800) 639-3111
ph: (603) 726-3800   fax: (603) 726-3870
www.transfertechnology.com

Wide Format Printers

GCC Printers
209 Burlington Rd
Bedford, MA 01730
(800) 942-3233 Ext 8733
fax: (800) 442-2329
www.gccprinters.com

OYO Instruments Inc
9777 West Gulf Bank Ste #10
Houston, TX 77040
(800) 747-7651
ph: (713) 937-5800   fax: (713) 937-1161
www.oyo.com

Vellum

Caseys' Page Mill Ltd
6528 South Oneida Ct
Englewood, CO 80111-4617
ph: (303) 220-1463
www.caseyspm.com

SMR Software
32 Northwest Fourth St
Grand Rapids, MN 55744
ph: (218) 326-0890   fax: (218)326-0984

Artists

Alice Flynn
www.aliceflynn.com

All West Graphics
46 - 2005 Boucherie Rd
Westbank , BC V4T1R4 Canada
ph: (250) 768-6905   fax: (250) 768-6905
www.allwestgraphics.com

Dave Moore Independent Artist
ph: (928) 443-1856
ph: (520) 899-7054
www.cableone.net/rioja/

Donny Vogler Graphic Art & Illustation
5982 Robinhood Rd
Pfafftown, NC 27040
dvgraphics.homestead.com/homepage.html

Echo
2437 Chestnut Dr
Little Elm, TX 75068
ph: (214) 502-1892
www.electrigrafix.com

Fishboy Fine Fishy Designs
9 Aerial St.
Arlington, MA 02474
(866) FLAT-ALE
ph: (781) 646-6474   fax: (786) 513-8294
www.fishboy.com

Magic Works Studio
10, Jalan 99, Kawasan 19,
Jalan Kapar Batu2,
41400, Klang, Selangor
Malaysia
ph: +(603) 3342-2603
ph: +(603) 3344-8871
www.magicworksart.com

Mark Smith Illustrations
www.coax.net/people/marcus714/menu.html

Michael Williams
PO Box 15
Belfast, ME 04915
www.michael-williams.com

Monster Graphics
ph: (858) 775-3648   fax: (858) 860-6400 x5463
www.monstergraphics.net

Night Owl Graphics
www.nightowlgraphics.com

Oakstone Studio
www.oakstonestudio.com

One Graphics Studios
One Graphics Studios
1530 Krameria St # 106
Denver, CO 80220-1558
ph: (303) 355 8583
www.onegraphics.com/index.html

Slickster
Kevin Mattoon
Dallas,TX
ph: (972) 293-0389
www.slickster.com/contact.htm

Steve McDonald
317 Ashwood
Azle, TX 76020
ph: (817) 221-3833
www.usscreen.com/steve

Studio Ink
hometown.aol.com/leeannvonr/studioink.html

Venture Studios
(219) 563-2887
www.bobbrownstudios.com

WIK Design
WIK DESIGN
PO Box 467
Baker, MT 59313
ph: (406) 778-2390   fax: (406) 778-3390
www.wikdesign.com

WX Color Mixer T-shirt Design Studio
www.wxcolormixer.com

Embroidery

Data Stitch, Inc
11255 Hwy 80 West #102
Aledo, TX 76008
(800) 765-1004
wwdatastitch.com

Embroidery University
Administration, Registration and Research coordinated through
Universal Design, Inc
Louisville, KY 40201-0278
ph: (502) 366-4100   fax: (502) 366-0444
www.embroideryuniversity.com

Imagination technology Inc.
571 Shoreveiw Park Rd
Shoreview, MN 55126
(800) 420-8125
ph: (651) 482-8125   fax: (651) 765-0041
www.embroideryplanet.com

Melco
1575 W 124th Ave
Denver, CO 80233
ph: (303) 457-1234   fax: (303) 252-0508
www.melco.com

Tajima America Corp
550 Commerce St
Franklin Lakes, NJ 07417-1310
ph: (201) 405-1201   fax: (201) 405-1205
www.tajima.com

Assorted Products

A.G.A.S. Car Flags
US Office (Main)
A.G.A.S.
295 E 8th St
New York, NY 10009
ph: (212) 777-6678   fax: (212) 202-4830
www.carflag.com

Bag Works
ph: (800) 365-7423   fax: (800) 678-7364
ph: (817) 446-8080   fax: (817) 446-8105
www.bagworks.com

Bevenco National Equipment Leasing
10101 Southwest Freeway Ste 330
Houston, TX 77074
(800) 683-7106
fax: (713) 772-5936
www.cogweb.com/bevenco

Excel Model Products Inc
Florida
ph: (727) 942-7740   fax: (727) 942-9600
www.excelmolded.com

Foster Manufacturing Company
905 Louis Dr
Warminster, PA 18974
(800) 523-4855
ph: (215) 442-1700   fax: (215) 442-1313
www.fostermfg.com

ILS Cutting
Integrated Laser Systems Inc
1460 Ventura Dr Ste #B
Cumming, GA 30040
ph: (770) 888-3808   fax: (770) 888-3803

Innovative Environmental Prod
PO Box 27608
Tempe, AZ 85285
(800) 847-3527
ph: (480) 921-4375
www.iepinc.com

McMaster-Carr
6100 Fulton Industrial Blvd / PO Box 740100
Atlanta, GA 30374
ph: (404) 346-7000   fax: (404) 349-9091
www.mcmaster.com

Mousepadvertising
PO Box 215
S Bound Brook, NJ 08880
(877) 292-3100
www.mousepadvertising.com

Pacific Coast Bach Label Company
1019 S Santa Fe
Los Angeles, CA 90021
(800) 394-4455
fax: (213) 629-4465
www.bachlabel.net

PSP Parmele Screen Process Supplies
13105 Saticoy St
North Hollywood, CA 91605
(800) 223-4PSP

Z Manufacturing Inc
222 N Main
Piedmont, MO 63957
(800) 348-2247
fax: (573) 223-7336
www.clearwatermfg.com

Find a number or address that does not work? Let us know 800-311-8962 or e-mail tshirt@homecashbusiness.com.

Know a company that should be on this list? Let us know 800-311-8962 or e-mail tshirt@homecashbusiness.com.

Included Screen-printing Supplies and Recommendations

SOY SOLVENT
To clean ink off of screens. Biodegradable and odorless. (800) 311-8962

DEGREASER
Neutralize 0246 fabric degreaser. Mixes 4:1 with water. (800) 753-5095

RECLAIMER
ER/35 concentrated emulsion remover. Mixes 5:1 with water. (800) 753-5095

EMULSION - Prochem WR-3 works great. (800) 753-5095

High-quality affordable Laser Vellum. Call (800) 640-2768 for info.

T-shirts and Apparel - www.cottonconnection.com

"How to Print T-Shirts for Fun and Profit" by Scott Fresner.
It's the best book on silk-screening website: www.usscreen.com.

NazDar Ink (800) 258-5050 in California. Ask for the location nearest you.
NazDar also carries ink for other products (stickers, plastic, wood etc.)

McLogins in Los Angeles (213) 749-2262. They also have stores in Anaheim, CA and San Diego, CA. They carry everything.

Murina www.murina.com All Styles A&G sports for great t-shirts at a good price plus they carry some supplies. California (800) 225-1364, Chicago (800) 621-6578, Atlanta Georgia (800) 421-1083, Buffalo NY All American supply (716) 882-4426.

Coast Graphics in Van Nuys, CA. They ship anywhere. Ask for JIM (800) 356-8866. Atlanta GA, OH, and NC (tell him where you saw this he has great prices) call Anthony (800) 948-4344.

Kelly Paper in CA, NV, and AZ now sells silkscreen supplies and velum (29 LB translucent #gn2911, $40 for ream of 500). They also carry the emulsion I use by the gallon. They ship nationwide. Call to for locations and to order (800) 675-3559.

ormation can be obtained at www.ICGtesting.com
he USA
223110215
8 V00002B/126/P

9 780595 478644